ROYAL COURT

GW00578146

Royal Court Theatre presents

ALASKA

by **DC Moore**

First performance at the Royal Court Jerwood Theatre Upstairs,
Sloane Square, London on 24 May 2007.

DC Moore

Alaska

Methuen Drama

Published by Methuen Drama 2007

1 3 5 7 9 10 8 6 4 2

Methuen Drama
A & C Black Publishers Limited
38 Soho Square
London W1D 3HB
www.acblack.com

ISBN: 978 0 713 68822 1

A CIP catalogue record for this book
is available from the British Library

Typeset by Country Setting, Kingsdown, Kent
Printed and bound in Great Britain by
MPG Books Ltd, Bodmin, Cornwall

ALASKA

by **DC Moore**

Adam **Sebastian Armesto**
Emma **Christine Bottomley**
Russell **Harry Hepple**
Chris **Thomas Morrison**
Frank **Rafe Spall**
Mamta **Fiona Wade**

Director **Maria Aberg**
Designer **Fred Meller**
Lighting Designer **David Holmes**
Sound Designer **Carolyn Downing**
Fight Director **Malcolm Ranson**
Assistant Director **Gbolahan Obisesan**
Casting **Amy Ball**
Production Manager **Sue Bird**
Stage Managers **Carla Archer, Sue Welch**
Dialect Coach **Jan Hayden Rowles**
Costume Supervisor **Fizz Jones**

The Royal Court and Stage Management wish to thank the following for their help with this production: Eagle Vending Services, www.safetysignsupplies.co.uk and vendingmachinequote.co.uk

THE COMPANY

DC Moore
DC Moore was part of the YWP writers' group in 2004/2005. Alaska received a reading as part of the Young Writers Festival 2007. This is his first play.

Maria Aberg (director)
For the Royal Court, as director: Angry Now (Latitude Festival).
For the Royal Court, as assistant director: Lucky Dog, Sweetest Swing in Baseball, The Sugar Syndrome.
Other theatre includes, as director: Days of Significance (RSC); Shrieks of Laughter (Soho Theatre); Stallerhof (Southwark Playhouse); Love and Money (Young Vic Studio); A Handful of Dust (Institute of Choreography and Dance); The Maids (Judi Dench Theatre). As associate director: The Winter's Tale, Pericles (RSC). As assistant director: The Crucible (RSC); Aristocrats (National); Shakespeare Love Songs (Globe, Neuss); Romeo and Juliet (Malmö Dramatic Theatre). Maria was a senior reader at the Royal Court for two years.

Sebastian Armesto
Theatre includes: Bedside Manners/Shock!/Taking Steps (Frinton and Sherringham Summer Theatres); The Taming of the Shrew (Cliveden Festival). Television includes: The Tudors, The Rise and Fall of Rome, The Impressionists, The Virgin Queen, Dr Who, The Bill, Hawking, The Famous Five. Film includes: Blood Monkeys, Losers Anonymous, Hymn (short), Marie Antoinette, A Feast at Midnight. Radio includes: More or Less.

Christine Bottomley
For the Royal Court: Ladybird.
Other theatre includes: Osama the Hero, A Single Act (Hampstead); Rutherford and Son (Royal Exchange, Manchester); Flush (Soho); The Pleasureman (Citizens'). Television includes: Sound, Sea of Souls, Instinct, The Innocence Project, Vincent, Blue Murder, The Street, Shameless, Caravaggio, Speeding, Murder Prevention, Sex Footballers & Videotape, Early Doors (series 1&2), Heartbeat, Burn It, Grease Monkeys, The Bill, Danziel and Pascoe, East Enders, Inspector Lynley Mysteries. Film includes: The Waiting Room, Venus, Death of a Socialist (short). Radio includes: Scissors and Ribbons, Money Magic.

Carolyn Downing (sound designer)
For the Royal Court, as associate sound designer: Forty Winks, O Go My Man (& Out of Joint). Other theatre includes, as sound designer: Angels in America: Millennium Approaches & Perestroika (Headlong Theatre); The Winter's Tale, Pericles, Days of Significance (RSC); A Whistle In The Dark, Moonshed (Royal Exchange, Manchester); Hysteria (Inspector Sands); Project D: I'm Mediocre (The Work Theatre Collective); Arsenic and Old Lace (Derby Playhouse);
The Water Engine (Theatre 503, in association with The Young Vic); Blood Wedding (Almeida); Gone To Earth (Shared Experience); Waiting For The Parade (Mountview); Habitats, Under The Curse (The Gate); Stallerhof, A Doll's House, The Double Bass, The Provoked Wife, Mongoose (Southwark Playhouse); The Watery Part of the World (Sound and Fury).
As associate sound designer: By the Bog of Cats (Wyndham's); The Overwhelming, Fix Up (National); Macbeth (Out of Joint).

Harry Hepple
Theatre includes: Been So Long (Stratford East/ RADA); A Doll's House, Othello, Sing Yer Hearts Out for the Lads, Widows, Assassins, Love's Comedy (RADA); Marat/Sade, Three Sisters, Romeo and Juliet, Bones (New College, Durham); Fine! Fine! Fine! (The Customs House); West Side Story (Gala Theatre, Durham).

David Holmes (lighting designer)
Theatre includes: Days of Significance (RSC Swan/ Davidson College, North Carolina); Cyrano de Bergerac, The Trestle at Pope Lick Creek, Harvey (Royal Exchange, Manchester); The Rise and Fall of Little Voice (Watermill); Tilt (Traverse, Edinburgh); Things of Dry Hours (The Gate/Royal Exchange, Manchester); Stallerhof (Southwark); Sweetness and Badness (Welsh National Opera Max); Cruising (Bush); The Vegemite Tales (The Venue); The Factory Girls, Lysistrata (Arcola); Tomorrow Morning (New End); L'Orfeo, The Beggar's Opera, The Threepenny Opera (Trinity College of Music); Fijis (South Bank Centre/The Place); The Leningrad Siege (Wilton's Music Hall); Woman In Mind, Be My Baby (Salisbury); Car Thieves (Birmingham); The Fantasticks, Ain't Misbehavin', House, Garden, Cleo Camping Emmanuelle and Dick (Harrogate); The Secret Rapture (Chichester); Twelfth Night (Cambridge); Look Back In Anger, The Mentalists (Exeter); The Water Engine, A State of Innocence (Theatre 503); Cosi fan Tutte (Guildhall School); The Tempest, The Sleeper's Den (Southwark).

Fred Meller (designer)
Theatre includes: Timon of Athens, Pericles (RSC/Cardboard Citizens'); The Fever, The Body of a Woman (Young Vic); Woyzeck (Riverside Studios/

tour); Richard III (KAOS); Storm2 (The Generating Co.); The Visitation of Mr Collioni (Salisbury/tour); Life With an Idiot (National/The Gate); Great Expectations (Unicorn/tour); Variety (Grid Iron/ Edinburgh International Festival); Caledonian Road, The Whiz Kid, Ghost Ward, A Warning to the Curious (Almeida); Epsom Downs, Telling Tales, A Taste of Honey (Nuffield, Southampton/tour); Mincemeat (Cardboard Citizens'); Death and the Maiden, Talking Heads, Skylight, The Rise and Fall of Little Voice (The Watermill); Othello, Rosencrantz and Guildenstern are Dead (Theatre Royal Bury St Edmunds/tour); David Copperfield (Eastern Angles tour); The Norman Conquests (Wolsey).
Exhibitions include: World Stage Design, Toronto 2005; The Prague Quadrennial 1999 and 2003, winning the golden Triga.
Awards include: The Jerwood Design Award; Year of the Artist Award; Arts Foundation Fellowship.

Thomas Morrison
Theatre includes: The History Boys (National/ Wyndham's/tour); On the Shore of the Wide World (Royal Exchange, Manchester/National); Kes (Royal Exchange, Manchester).
Television includes: The Bill, Oddsquad, Holby City, Blackpool.
Radio includes: Strike, Big Ears Learns to Listen, Dear Dr Goebbels.

Gbolahan Obisesan (assistant director)
As director, theatre includes: My Life (Croydon Warehouse); Exerpt of Tintin in Tibet (Young Vic/ Talawa); Hold it Up (Soho); Skipping Rope (Lowry Studio, Manchester); Roadside (Lyric Hammersmith Studio).
As assistant director, theatre includes: generations (Young Vic); Heat and Light (Hampstead); Astronaut Wives Club, 3 Days in July (Soho); The Shipwrights' Tale (NYT).

Malcolm Ranson (fight director)
Theatre includes: King Lear, Macbeth, Pericles, Hamlet, Don Carlos, The Plantaganets, Two Noble Kinsmen, Twelfth Night, Peter Pan, Cymbeline, Coriolanus, Last Days of Don Juan, Edward II, Julius Caesar, The Virtuoso, The Changeling, Fair Maid of the West, Richard III, Les Miserables, Troilus and Cressida, Clockwork Orange (RSC); Dinner, Coast of Utopia, The Relapse, Playboy of the Western World, Remembrance of Things Past, The Villain's Opera, Antony and Cleopatra, The Critic, Cymbeline, The Wind in the Willows, The Recruiting Officer, Macbeth, The Shaughraun, Hamlet, The Miser, An Inspector Calls, Rosencrantz and Guildenstern are Dead, Peter Pan, A View from the Bridge, Mutabilite, Flight, Peter Pan, Troilus and Cressida, Look Back in Anger, Private Lives (National); Not About Nightingales, Oklahoma! (National/Broadway); Lone Star Love (off

Broadway); Noises Off, Les Liaisons Dangereuses (RSC/West End); Woman in White, Bombay Dreams, La Cava (West End); The Three Musketeers (Holland/Berlin/Stuttgart); Dirty Dancing (Hamburg).
Opera includes: Carmen, Faust, The Force of Destiny (ENO); Don Giovanni (Opera 80); Simon Boccanegra, The Second Mrs Kong (Glyndebourne); The Poisoned Chalice (Music Theatre London); Don Giovanni (Salzburg Festival); Julius Caesar (Staatspiele, Munich).
Television includes: By the Sword Divided, Casualty, The Vorpal Blade, Black Adder, Submariners, Howard's Way, Henry IV, Nightingales, Macbeth, Titus Andronicus, Richard III, Henry VI parts I, II and III.
Film includes: Oklahoma!, Jesus Christ Superstar, Edward II, A Feast of July, Twelfth Night.

Rafe Spall
For the Royal Court: Just a Bloke.
Other theatre includes: John Gabriel Borkman (Donmar); The Knight of the Burning Pestle (Young Vic); Prayer for Owen Meany (National); Nicholas Nickelby (Lyric Hammersmith).
Television includes: Dracula, Wide Sargasso Sea, The Chatterley Affair, Cracker, The Romantics, The Rotters' Club, The Lion in Winter.
Film includes: Hot Fuzz, A Good Year, The Last Drop, Kidulthood, Green Street, Shaun of the Dead, The Calcium Kid, Out of Control.
Radio includes: The Real Thing, Hide.

Fiona Wade
Theatre includes: The Far Pavilions (Shaftesbury); Strictly Dandia (Edinburgh/Lyric Hammersmith); Miss Saigon (Malmö Opera och Musikteater); Aladdin (Theatre Royal, Nottingham); Inner City Jam (West Yorkshire Playhouse); West Side Story, Romeo & Juliet (Courtyard, Hereford); Miss Saigon (Theatre Royal, Drury Lane); Cinderella (Theatre Royal, Stratford East); Aladdin (Malvern).
Television includes: Wire in the Blood, Holby City, Where the Heart Is, Genie in the House, Doctors, Holy Smoke, 24Seven, Grange Hill.

14 June – 21 July

ROYAL COURT

the pain and the itch

AN INFECTIOUS COMEDY

by Bruce Norris

A cosy family Thanksgiving dinner for six. Someone – or something – is leaving bite marks in the avocados. Clay and Kelly's daughter Kayla has an itch and Carol can't remember who played Gandhi.

In his first UK production, American writer Bruce Norris takes a withering look at phoney liberal values in this hilarious social satire.

Direction
Dominic Cooke

Design
Robert Innes Hopkins

Lighting
Hugh Vanstone

Sound
Paul Arditti

Cast includes
Matthew Macfadyen

500 tickets
£5 for 25s
and under*

020 7565 5000
www.royalcourttheatre.com
Royal Court Theatre, Sloane Square, London SW1

ARTS COUNCIL ENGLAND

AWARDS FOR
THE ROYAL COURT

Martin McDonagh's The Beauty Queen of Leenane (co-production with Druid Theatre Company) won four 1998 Tony Awards including Garry Hynes for Best Director. Eugene Ionesco's The Chairs (co-production with Theatre de Complicite) was nominated for six Tony awards. David Hare won the 1998 Time Out Live Award for Outstanding Achievement and six awards in New York including the Drama League, Drama Desk and New York Critics Circle Award for Via Dolorosa. Sarah Kane won the 1998 Arts Foundation Fellowship in Playwriting. Rebecca Prichard won the 1998 Critics' Circle Award for Most Promising Playwright for Yard Gal (co-production with Clean Break).

Conor McPherson won the 1999 Olivier Award for Best New Play for The Weir. The Royal Court won the 1999 ITI Award for Excellence in International Theatre. Sarah Kane's Cleansed was judged Best Foreign Language Play in 1999 by Theater Heute in Germany. Gary Mitchell won the 1999 Pearson Best Play Award for Trust. Rebecca Gilman was joint winner of the 1999 George Devine Award and won the 1999 Evening Standard Award for Most Promising Playwright for The Glory of Living.

In 1999, the Royal Court won the European theatre prize New Theatrical Realities, presented at Taormina Arte in Sicily, for its efforts in recent years in discovering and producing the work of young British dramatists.

Roy Williams and Gary Mitchell were joint winners of the George Devine Award 2000 for Most Promising Playwright for Lift Off and The Force of Change respectively. At the Barclays Theatre Awards 2000 presented by the TMA, Richard Wilson won the Best Director Award for David Gieselmann's Mr Kolpert and Jeremy Herbert won the Best Designer Award for Sarah Kane's 4.48 Psychosis. Gary Mitchell won the Evening Standard's Charles Wintour Award 2000 for Most Promising Playwright for The Force of Change. Stephen Jeffreys' I Just Stopped by to See the Man won an AT&T: On Stage Award 2000.

David Eldridge's Under the Blue Sky won the Time Out Live Award 2001 for Best New Play in the West End. Leo Butler won the George Devine Award 2001 for Most Promising Playwright for Redundant. Roy Williams won the Evening Standard's Charles Wintour Award 2001 for Most Promising Playwright for Clubland. Grae Cleugh won the 2001 Olivier Award for Most Promising Playwright for Fucking Games.

Richard Bean was joint winner of the George Devine Award 2002 for Most Promising Playwright for Under the Whaleback. Caryl Churchill won the 2002 Evening Standard Award for Best New Play for A Number. Vassily Sigarev won the 2002 Evening

Standard Charles Wintour Award for Most Promising Playwright for Plasticine. Ian MacNeil won the 2002 Evening Standard Award for Best Design for A Number and Plasticine. Peter Gill won the 2002 Critics' Circle Award for Best New Play for The York Realist (English Touring Theatre). Ché Walker won the 2003 George Devine Award for Most Promising Playwright for Flesh Wound. Lucy Prebble won the 2003 Critics' Circle Award and the 2004 George Devine Award for Most Promising Playwright, and the TMA Theatre Award 2004 for Best New Play for The Sugar Syndrome. Richard Bean won the 2005 Critics' Circle Award for Best New Play for Harvest. Laura Wade won the 2005 Critics' Circle Award for Most Promising Playwright and the 2005 Pearson Best Play Award for Breathing Corpses. The 2006 Whatsonstage Theatregoers' Choice Award for Best New Play was won by My Name is Rachel Corrie. The 2005 Evening Standard Special Award was given to the Royal Court 'for making and changing theatrical history this last half century'.

Tom Stoppard's Rock 'n' Roll won the 2006 Evening Standard Award for Best Play and the 2006 Critics' Circle Award for Best Play. Lucy Caldwell won the 2006 George Devine Award and a Special Award in the 2007 Susan Smith Blackburn Awards for Leaves.

ROYAL COURT BOOKSHOP

The Royal Court bookshop offers a range of contemporary plays and publications on the theory and practice of modern drama. The staff specialise in assisting with the selection of audition monologues and scenes. Royal Court playtexts from past and present productions cost £2.
The Bookshop is situated to the right of the stairs leading to the ROYAL COURT CAFE BAR.

Monday to Friday 3 – 10pm
Saturday 2.30 – 10pm
(Closed shortly every evening from 7.45 to 8.15pm)

For information tel: 020 7565 5024
or email: bookshop@royalcourttheatre.com

Books can also be ordered from our website
www.royalcourttheatre.com

THE ENGLISH STAGE COMPANY AT THE ROYAL COURT

The English Stage Company at the Royal Court opened in 1956 as a subsidised theatre producing new British plays, international plays and some classical revivals.

The first artistic director George Devine aimed to create a writers' theatre, 'a place where the dramatist is acknowledged as the fundamental creative force in the theatre and where the play is more important than the actors, the director, the designer'. The urgent need was to find a contemporary style in which the play, the acting, direction and design are all combined. He believed that 'the battle will be a long one to continue to create the right conditions for writers to work in'.

Devine aimed to discover 'hard-hitting, uncompromising writers whose plays are stimulating, provocative and exciting'. The Royal Court production of John Osborne's Look Back in Anger in May 1956 is now seen as the decisive starting point of modern British drama and the policy created a new generation of British playwrights. The first wave included John Osborne, Arnold Wesker, John Arden, Ann Jellicoe, N F Simpson and Edward Bond. Early seasons included new international plays by Bertolt Brecht, Eugène Ionesco, Samuel Beckett and Jean-Paul Sartre.

The theatre started with the 400-seat proscenium arch Theatre Downstairs, and in 1969 opened a second theatre, the 60-seat studio Theatre Upstairs. Some productions transfer to the West End, such as Tom Stoppard's Rock 'n' Roll, My Name is Rachel Corrie, Terry Johnson's Hitchcock Blonde, Caryl Churchill's Far Away and Conor McPherson's The Weir. Recent touring productions include Sarah Kane's 4.48 Psychosis (US tour) and Ché Walker's Flesh Wound (Galway Arts Festival). The Royal Court also co-produces plays which transfer to the West End or tour internationally, such as Conor McPherson's Shining City (with Gate Theatre, Dublin), Sebastian Barry's The Steward of Christendom and Mark Ravenhill's Shopping and Fucking (with Out of Joint), Martin McDonagh's The Beauty Queen Of Leenane (with Druid), Ayub Khan Din's East is East (with Tamasha).

Since 1994 the Royal Court's artistic policy has again been vigorously directed to finding and producing a new generation of playwrights. The writers include Joe Penhall, Rebecca Prichard, Michael Wynne, Nick Grosso, Judy Upton, Meredith Oakes, Sarah Kane, Anthony Neilson, Judith Johnson, James Stock, Jez Butterworth, Marina Carr, Phyllis Nagy, Simon Block, Martin McDonagh, Mark Ravenhill, Ayub Khan Din, Tamantha Hammerschlag,

photo: Stephen Cummiiskey

Jess Walters, Ché Walker, Conor McPherson, Simon Stephens, Richard Bean, Roy Williams, Gary Mitchell, Mick Mahoney, Rebecca Gilman, Christopher Shinn, Kia Corthron, David Gieselmann, Marius von Mayenburg, David Eldridge, Leo Butler, Zinnie Harris, Grae Cleugh, Roland Schimmelpfennig, Chloe Moss, DeObia Oparei, Enda Walsh, Vassily Sigarev, the Presnyakov Brothers, Marcos Barbosa, Lucy Prebble, John Donnelly, Clare Pollard, Robin French, Elyzabeth Gregory Wilder, Rob Evans, Laura Wade, Debbie Tucker Green, Levi David Addai, Simon Farquhar, Bola Agbaje, Alexandra Wood, Lucy Caldwell, Polly Stenham, Mike Bartlett and DC Moore. This expanded programme of new plays has been made possible through the support of A.S.K. Theater Projects and the Skirball Foundation, The Jerwood Charity, the American Friends of the Royal Court Theatre and (in 1994/5 and 1999) the National Theatre Studio.

The refurbished theatre in Sloane Square opened in February 2000, with a policy still inspired by the first artistic director George Devine. The Royal Court is an international theatre for new plays and new playwrights, and the work shapes contemporary drama in Britain and overseas.

The Royal Court's long and successful history of innovation has been built by generations of gifted and imaginative individuals. For information on the many exciting ways you can help support the theatre, please contact the Development Department on 020 7565 5079.

PROGRAMME SUPPORTERS

The Royal Court (English Stage Company Ltd) receives its principal funding from Arts Council England, London. It is also supported financially by a wide range of private companies, charitable and public bodies, and earns the remainder of its income from the box office and its own trading activities.

The Genesis Foundation supports the Royal Court's work with International Playwrights.

The Jerwood Charity supports new plays by new playwrights through the Jerwood New Playwrights series.

The Artistic Director's Chair is supported by a lead grant from The Peter Jay Sharp Foundation, contributing to the activities of the Artistic Director's office. Over the past nine years the BBC has supported the Gerald Chapman Fund for directors.

American Friends of the Royal Court are primarily focused on raising funds to enable the theatre to produce new work by emerging American writers. AFRCT has also supported the participation of young artists in the Royal Court's acclaimed International Residency. Contact: 001-212-946-5724.

FOR THE ROYAL COURT

Artistic Director **Dominic Cooke**
Associate Director International **Elyse Dodgson**
Associate Directors **Ramin Gray, Emily McLaughlin,
Sacha Wares**
Casting Director **Amy Ball**
Literary Associate **Terry Johnson***
Pearson Playwright **Mike Bartlett**†
International Administrator **Chris James**
Trainee Director **Lyndsey Turner**
Artistic Assistant **Rebecca Hanna-Grindall**
International Assistant **William Drew**

Production Manager **Paul Handley**
Deputy Production Manager **Sue Bird**
Production Assistant **Sarah Davies**
Head of Lighting **Johanna Town**
Lighting Assistants **Nicki Brown, Kelli Zezulka**
Lighting Board Operator **Stephen Andrews**
Head of Stage **Steven Stickler**
Stage Deputy **Daniel Lockett**
Stage Chargehand **Lee Crimmen**
Head of Sound **Ian Dickinson**
Sound Deputy **Emma Laxton**
Acting Head of Costume **Jackie Orton**

YOUNG WRITERS PROGRAMME
Associate Director **Ola Animashawun**
Administrator **Nina Lyndon**
Outreach Worker **Lucy Dunkerley**
Writers' Tutor **Leo Butler***

General Manager **Diane Borger**
Administrator **Oliver Rance**
Acting Head of Finance **Helen Perryer**
Finance Officer **Rachel Harrison***
Finance Officer **Martin Wheeler**

Head of Communications **Kym Bartlett**
Marketing Manager **Kelly Duffy**
Press Officer **Stephen Pidcock**
Audience Development Officer **Gemma Frayne**
Marketing Intern **Charlotte Barnes**

Sales Manager **David Kantounas**
Deputy Sales Manager **Stuart Grey**
Box Office Sales Assistants **Daniel Alicandro,
Annet Ferguson, Sonia Smith**

Head of Development **Nicky Jones**
Development Consultant (maternity cover)
Caroline Hawley
Senior Development Manager **Gaby Styles**
Development Manager **Hannah Clifford**

Theatre Manager **Bobbie Stokes**
Front of House Managers **Nathalie Meghriche,
Lucinda Springett**
Bar and Food Manager **Darren Elliott**
Deputy Bar and Food Manager **Claire Simpson**
Duty House Managers **Charlie Revell***, **Matt Wood***
Bookshop Manager **Simon David**
Assistant Bookshop Manager **Edin Suljic***
Bookshop Assistants **Helen Bennett***, **Fiona Clift***
Building Maintenance Administrator **Jon Hunter**
Stage Door/Reception **Simon David***,
Paul Lovegrove, Tyrone Lucas

Thanks to all of our box office assistants, ushers
and bar staff.

* Part-time.

† This theatre has the support of the Pearson Playwrights' scheme,
sponsored by the Peggy Ramsay Foundation.

ENGLISH STAGE COMPANY

President
Sir John Mortimer CBE QC

Vice President
Dame Joan Plowright CBE

Honorary Council
Sir Richard Eyre CBE
Alan Grieve CBE
Martin Paisner CBE

Council
Chairman **Anthony Burton**
Vice Chairman **Graham Devlin**

Members
Jennette Arnold
Judy Daish
Sir David Green KCMG
Joyce Hytner OBE
Tamara Ingram
Stephen Jeffreys
Phyllida Lloyd
James Midgley
Sophie Okonedo
Anita Scott
Katharine Viner
Stewart Wood

Alaska

Characters

Frank, *twenty-four*
Adam, *eighteen*
Russell, *eighteen*
Emma, *twenty-three*
Mamta, *nineteen*
Chris, *seventeen*

Part One

Scene One

December. **Frank**'s *bedroom in halls of residence at university.* **Frank** *is in bed.*

We hear some drunken commotion from outside in the hallway. Then **Adam***, shushing aggressively and saying 'Shut up' repeatedly under his breath.*

Knocking at the door.

Silence.

More knocking, before the door opens and **Adam** *peers round. He is drunk.*

Adam (*half-whisper*) Frank? Frank? (*Louder.*) *Frank.*

Frank (*still half asleep*) What?

Adam I know it's late but can we get some . . . cannabis?

Frank (*still half asleep*) What you doing?

Adam Got the money. Be dead quick, mate.

Pause. **Frank** *turns a lamp on.*

Frank Do you know how late it is?

Adam*, who is smoking, comes into the room.* **Frank** *sits up on his bed.*

Adam We got pizza in the kitchen, mate, if you want some.

No response.

So, is an eighth gonna be alright?

Frank *shrugs an offhand 'Yes'.*

Adam Cool. How much is that gonna be exactly?

Frank Forty.

Adam Pounds?

Frank *nods and takes a swig from a two-litre bottle of water by his bed.*

Adam   Simon's sister can get us that much for like . . . twenty quid. That's all we've got.

Frank   Supply, mate. Demand, mate.

Adam   Right.

Frank   Though actually. Maybe. Maybe I could go into your room, steal a moment or two with your lady. Make up the shortfall. Called Anna, in't she? I see her down the library . . .

Adam   Is it skunk or weed?

Frank   Yeah, see her all the time, the library.

Adam   Is it . . . skunk / or?

Frank   Beavering away. It's solid. Helps me study.

Adam   Really? Always makes me a bit . . .

Frank   You're never with her. Are ya?

Adam   Can barely read, let alone some. Textbook.

Frank   Cos I wouldn't let her out of my sight. Peach like that.

Silence.

Alright. How 'bout, how 'bout you give me an essay?

Adam (*not understanding*)   Right.

Frank   Just to read. No one ever shows nothing. To me. You do history. I seen ya. I like history. So. An essay and twenty quid and we're done.

Adam   Um. OK.

Adam*'s cigarette has run out. He looks around, before casually putting it out in the water bottle.* **Frank** *smiles with disgust.* **Adam** *smiles back, exits.*

A pause before **Frank** *takes the water bottle and inspects it. Puts the top back on it. Shakes it. Looks at it, holds it up, watching the fag end floating round.*

Adam *returns with an essay, offers it to* **Frank**.

Frank *takes the essay and starts reading.* **Adam** *passes him the money.* **Frank** *pockets it, continues to read.* **Adam** *watches* **Frank**, *perplexed, waiting for some sign of cannabis.*

Adam   Can we just . . . ? Can I just . . . ?

Frank   Can you just . . . ?

Adam   Get the . . . the drugs. Everyone's in the kitchen. Waiting.

Frank   But I ain't finished.

Adam   Well, can you not read it like . . . later?

Frank   That wasn't the agreement, mate. I'm not a bank.

Frank *goes back to reading.*

Adam   But . . .

Annoyed but accepting that he will have to wait, **Adam** *relaxes. Takes in the room, sees an open Bible, which he picks up, reads.*

Silence.

Frank *(having read three paragraphs or so, genuinely impressed)*   This. Seems. Very. Very good.

Adam   Yeah?

Frank   Your prose. It's very. Clear. Precise. I mean, this a fucking good intro. Can I keep it? Finish it?

Adam   If you want.

Frank   Great.

He smiles at **Adam**, *briefly forgetting why* **Adam** *is in his room.*

Adam   Are you gonna . . . ?

Frank   Oh. Yeah. Course. Sorry, mate. Forget me head.

Frank *gets out a small wooden box from under his bed.*

Frank   You wanna be an academic then, or . . . ? Look like you got the, the smarts for it.

As they talk **Frank** *opens the box, takes out a little hunting knife and cannabis resin.*

Adam   No. Wanna do something different. You know. Like, media stuff. (*Referencing Bible.*) Do you *really* believe in all this? I know you're very . . .

Frank   How d'ya mean, 'different'?

He begins cutting the eighth.

Adam   Yeah, my dad's. Erm. Professor.

Frank   Of . . . ?

Adam   History.

Frank   Right. That's gotta be. Useful.

Adam   Yeah, he's always emailing me, helping me out, you know?

Frank   Helping out?

Adam (*referencing Bible*)   So do you believe in miracles / and – ?

Frank   Helping out with what?

Adam (*gestures towards the essay in* **Frank**'*s hands*)   On the. With the essays.

Frank *twigs.*

Frank   That's a fucking. That's. (*Gesturing to the essay.*) So let's get this straight, you didn't even . . . ?

Adam   What? It's first year. Doesn't count. And . . . and Dad didn't write *all of it*. He just gets . . . got. Excited. Thought of the title and then. Wrote. Some of it. You know what dads are like.

Frank   Not really.

Adam   How d'ya mean?

Frank   Lost mine. Falklands.

Adam   Shit.

Frank   Yeah.

Adam   How did he . . . how did he . . . ?

Frank   What?

Adam   Die. Was it in . . . combat?

Frank   What? What you talking about? Course it was.

Adam (*puts the Bible down*)   Must be very hard to . . . to have to, deal with that.

Frank   Yeah. But I do, you know? I do. I deal with it. Every day. Whereas, what you ever dealt with, yeah? I mean, coming in here. You're just a . . . a kid. A fucking . . . Adam. Adam, mate. Do you know how many times you've knocked on that door?

Adam *shrugs.*

Frank   Twice. Other time. You wanted some Rizlas.

Adam   Right?

Frank   Twice. In four months.

Adam   Yeah, well, I'm not being funny but when you came out with us in Freshers' Week you told Priya she was going to Hell. You know? What is that?

Frank   That's not exactly what I said, mate. Don't be –

Adam   And all that shit about sewing people up inside pigs. D'ya not get that maybe that's a bit rude?

Frank *stands, still holding the knife from cutting gear.*

Frank   What about you cheating me out of a degree I paid good money for by copying off your posh cunt dad?

No response.

I didn't work and save for three years to go clubbing with Pakis.

Adam   Right. Right, can I just get the gear?

No response.

OK. Will you just give me the money?

Frank   Sorry. We don't do cashback.

Adam *visibly begins to sober.*

Adam   Just cos you're poor doesn't mean you're hard.

Frank   Just cos you're a cunt doesn't make you a cunt.

Adam   Right. Is that the sound of the streets?

Frank   Why don't you and your haircut fuck off out my room?

Knocking at the door, which is now slightly ajar.

Russell (*off*)   Adam? Adam? Adam, mate?

Adam   Yeah?

Enter **Russell***. He is white but blacked up, dressed to look like Mr T.*

Russell   You alright, mate? How ya doing? Dave just lit one of his farts in the kitchen. Massive flame. Yeah? Like – (*Makes impressive explosion sound and gesture.*) You got the gear, mate?

Adam   It's all good, mate.

Russell   Wicked, mate. You alright, mate?

Frank   . . .

Russell   *Yeah.* Thanks for the gear, mate. Sorry if we woke you up. (*As Mr T.*) 'I pity the fool who wakes Frank up! I ain't gonna get on no plane! Damn fool!' (*No response.*) You having a good night, mate?

Frank   Just got worse, to be honest.

Russell (*not registering*)   I licked sambuca off this girl's belly. Then, I fingered her in the bar. Was awesome. Got a picture of her boobs, like, on my phone.

He laughs.

Silence.

Cool. Just gonna go and, er. Have a. A dump. Thanks for the er . . . the ganja, Frank. You're a good man, yeah? You're alright. (*To* **Adam**.) See ya back in the kitchen in a bit, mate, yeah?

Adam *nods.*

Russell *exits, bellowing 'I pity the fool! Damn fool!' as he goes down the hallway before slipping into a Bo' Selecta Michael Jackson impression.*

Pause.

Frank   What does he study?

Adam   Politics.

Pause. **Adam** *moves towards the gear,* **Frank** *puts himself in the way.* **Adam** *reaches anyway.* **Frank** *threatens with his knife and pushes him with his other arm.* **Adam** *swiftly and expertly takes* **Frank**'s *knife-carrying arm and twists it behind his back while pushing him to the ground.* **Frank** *struggles but the pain is too much.*

Adam   Tell you what. While we're getting all. Manly. You talk shit like that about Anna again and I will fucking hurt you.

Frank   Do your worst, you . . .

Adam *gives a quick and painful twist of* **Frank**'s *arm and leans in towards him.*

Frank *grunts with pain.*

Adam   Look, why don't you just crawl back to your little estate?

Frank (*through gritted teeth, determined*)   There's this black geezer. She's very friendly with. *Anna.* In the library.

Adam *delivers a violent twist which is close to breaking* **Frank**'s *arm.*

Frank   Arh! I'm sorry. I'm sorry! Just stop, mate. You're gonna. FUCK.

Content that **Frank** *is beaten,* **Adam** *releases the pressure on his arm.* **Adam** *stands up, picks up the gear and goes to exit.*

Adam (*remembering, turning back*)   Actually. Do you have any Rizlas?

Frank *is still face down on the floor, breathing deeply.*

Frank   Top drawer.

Adam *goes to the drawer, takes a packet of Rizlas.*

Adam   Awesome.

He exits.

Silence.

We hear cheers from the kitchen as **Adam** *returns, drugs in hand.*

Blackout.

Scene Two

February of the following year. A Tuesday afternoon. The staffroom of a multiplex cinema. **Emma**, *who is wearing her cinema uniform, is eating an apple and reading a newspaper. In the background,* The Simpsons *is on a TV/video combination, which is fitted high in a corner of the room.*

Enter **Mamta**.

As she has her back to her, **Emma** *hasn't noticed* **Mamta**, *who is unsure of how best to get* **Emma**'s *attention.*

Silence.

Emma *stands up to fetch something from her coat. She gets a fright as she sees* **Mamta**.

Emma   *Jesus wept.* Where'd you sneak up from?

Mamta   Um. / Martin said –

Emma (*not listening*)   Sorry, take it ya realise this is the staffroom? As much as this does look like Screen Five, I'm not actually, believe it or not, Sigourney fucking Weaver.

Mamta   Yeah, I just –

Emma   So do you mind going back out through the double doors, and turning left, yeah? Better hurry, cos you only got about another minute or two of previews left before it starts. Well, go on. Toddle on then.

Silence.

Are you deaf or summat? Do. You. Mind. Going. / Back out –

Mamta   I *work* here.

Emma   What?

Mamta   I'm starting tomorrow. Had an interview last week and they told me to come in today to get my uniform.

Emma   Oh. Right. (*Realising.*) Shit. *Shit.* You're. You must be. Saw your name on the rota, thought it were new. You're . . . (*Struggling to remember her name.*) . . . Mumra?

Mamta   Not quite. Erm. Mamta.

Emma   Sorry?

Mamta   Mamta.

Emma   Mamtra?

Mamta   Mam-*ta*.

Emma   Mam-tar?

Mamta   Mamta.

Emma (*nods*)   Right. Right. Could you just, could you just say it one more time and a little bit slower for me? Is that alright? Sorry, you don't mind, do ya?

Mamta   No. It's fine. It's. Right. It's. Mam. Ta. Mamta.

Pause.

Emma   Mamta?

Mamta   That's the one.

Emma   Lovely. (*Pause.*) What kinda name is that?

Mamta   It's mine.

Emma   Oh. Anyway. I'm. Emma. (*Making a joke, as if having to explain how it is pronounced.*) Em-ma.

Mamta *nods and tries a smile.*

Emma   It's a pretty exotic name. Emma. Everyone at school was dead jealous. (*Pause.*) Sorry for being a bit . . . *off* with ya, when you came in. We just get a load of gyppos coming back here, scabbing about, looking for shit to nick. Though obviously you're not one.

Mamta   Gyppos?

Emma   Yeah. Do you not see 'em at the bottom of the car park? Twice a year they rock up. Regular as fuck. We lost three tellies and a kettle last year. And a life-size cut-out of Will Smith. (*Pause.*) Where they putting ya?

Mamta   Box office.

Emma   Oh, you'll be right then. You mainly have to deal with 'em – gyppos – when you're on kiosk. They always come in scouting for toffee popcorn.

Mamta   Right.

Emma   I work on bar. Upstairs.

Mamta   Could I just get my uniform? I kinda have to be somewhere.

Emma   Oh, yeah. Course. What colour?

Mamta   Sorry?

Emma   You got three options. Yellow. Blue. Red. For your top. Which do you want?

Mamta   Erm. (*Gesturing to* **Emma**'s *blue worktop.*) Blue?

Emma (*moving towards the door as she speaks*) Ooh, good choice, madam. Right, now wait here and I'll just go and get one for ya. I'll do me best to grab a new one, cos sometimes they do try and fob you off with some old second-hand musky bastard

and it'll have a load of stains on it, which look like and –
thinking about some of the people who work here – probably
actually are. Semen. So, wish me luck you don't get a spunky
one.

Emma *exits.*

Mamta (*after her*)   Erm. Good luck.

Emma (*off*)   Cheers. Take a seat and I'll be back in a minute.

Mamta *takes in the staffroom but doesn't sit down.*

Blackout.

Scene Three

*The same day as Scene Two. Early evening. Outside the delivery doors of
the cinema, overlooking a car park, which serves a large retail park.*

*Note: the delivery doors are also a fire exit. This means that, whenever
anyone goes for a smoke, a brick must be wedged into the door to stop the
smokers getting locked out. So these doors are ajar for nearly every scene.*

Frank, *wearing the uniform of the cinema, is smoking and drinking a
can of Diet Coke. Lost in thought.*

Enter **Chris**, *also wearing the cinema uniform.*

Frank *acknowledges* **Chris** *and* **Chris** *smiles back.*

Frank   Can I help you?

Chris   . . . ?

Frank   Am I needed, back inside?

Chris   No, I just, I just came out cos I thought you might
want some company on your break.

Frank   Right. Well, I'm alright, so . . .

Pause. **Frank** *takes a drag of his cigarette.*

Chris   Like it out here.

Pause.

Frank   Why's that?

Chris   The view.

Frank   The view?

Chris *gestures to the space in front of them.*

Frank   Would that be of the car park or all the caravans at the end of it?

Chris   No, of the sky. You get a big view of it out here, wide, cos there's no houses in the way. (*Referring to the sky above him.*) Can't see this much sky most places.

Frank   And that's good?

Chris   Course it is. But it's best in autumn.

Frank   Well, hopefully I won't be round that long.

Chris   Why, do you not like it here? Are you being bullied?

Frank   No. No, I just. Well, it's a bit. It's a bit shit, isn't it?

Chris   No. It's *brilliant*. You get to go see films for free. There's loads of free food. Everyone's really nice. And you get paid. And. You like Emma, I've seen you smiling with her, you *really* like her. And . . .

Frank   Alright, alright, you've convinced me. It's fucking brilliant, Chris, alright?

Chris *smiles.*

Pause.

Frank   Want a fag then?

Chris   Erm. OK.

Chris *takes a cigarette and* **Frank** *lights it for him. It's clear that* **Chris** *is not normally a smoker.*

Frank *is now looking up admiringly at the sky.*

Frank   'And God made two great lights: the greater light to rule the day, and the lesser light to rule the night.'

Chris   Is that religious?

Frank   Yeah. Genesis.

Chris   Like, from the Bible?

Frank   Chapter One. Verse Sixteen.

Chris   Sounds good.

Frank   Yeah. (*Pause.*) 'And God made two great lights: the greater light to rule the day, and the lesser light to rule the night.'

Chris   And it rhymes.

Frank *nods a little.*

Frank   It's great to memorise, you know? I was at uni for a bit, learnt whole chunks of it.

Pause. **Chris** *takes a drag, coughs a little.*

Frank *smiles, catches* **Chris**'s *eye.*

Chris   What?

Frank   You.

Chris   Why?

Frank   You're funny.

Chris   Why?

Frank   You do that dopey little cough every time you have a drag.

Chris   Do I?

He looks at **Frank** *before taking a determined drag. He holds his breath, trying not to cough. Fails with an outward breath.*

Chris   I don't think I did it before you said about it.

Frank   It's alright. You just gotta breathe it in a bit deeper. And slower as it comes out. How long you been smoking for?

Chris   I only coughed just then. I don't normally –

Frank   How many a, a day?

Chris   About. One.

Frank   Cos I been here a month now and I ain't seen you have one before.

Chris   I just like it.

Frank   Well, breathe it proper. Deep. If you're gonna do it, enjoy it, yeah? (*He demonstrates.*) Out.

Chris *copies him. Coughs again.*

Frank *smiles and, noticing that* **Chris** *is a bit despondent, takes a softer approach.*

Frank   Try it again.

Chris   No.

Frank   Please, go on. Just. Relax.

Chris   You're being horrible.

Frank   No, I'm not. I'm helping. (*Waiting till he has concrete eye contact with* **Chris**.) Just – in, two, three. Hold it, enjoy it. Out, two, three. Like it's air. But better. Come on.

Chris *takes a drag and with concentrated effort breathes out the smoke, managing to stifle his cough reflex.*

Frank   There we go. (*Toasts him with the can of Coke.*) To Chris.

Chris (*smiling*)   Idiot.

Frank *plays offended and playfully cuffs* **Chris** *on his arm.*

Frank   Well, this idiot's just been offered kiosk supervisor.

Chris   That's brilliant.

Frank   Martin just had a word. Extra quid-fifty an hour. And you get the shirt-and-tie number.

Chris   I'd like that. I'd love that. Hate baseball caps. Gets all sweaty when you're doing the hotdogs.

Frank   Told 'em I'd think it over.

Chris   You'd be a good boss.

Frank   That's not the . . . it's just that I'm better than . . .

Chris   Yeah, you are, but you could, you could get me so I don't ever have to do floor again. Don't like ushering. Drunk people saying, 'I don't care whose seat it is!' and calling me a 'wankstain'. But if you were the boss I could work with you on kiosk all the time and just make popcorn and . . .

Frank   Sorry, mate, but I'm, I'm too old to get excited about supervising people, cleaning . . . drink dispensers. Making nachos. I'm twenty-four, you know? Time is just. Fucking off. Leaving me with my dick up my arse.

Chris   But you're so clever, you'll be OK, won't you? Bet you it will all work out in the end. Just like it does in the Bible.

Frank   Maybe. I dunno. (*Sighing.*) *Fuck.*

Silence, during which he stubs out his cigarette.

Look, I better get off. (*Starting to go.*) See ya in a bit, yeah?

Chris   Could . . . ? Do you . . . ?

Frank   What?

Chris   Do you like . . . ?

Frank   What? (*Pause.*) What?

Chris   Would you like to go bowling?

Frank   I'm back on three minutes.

Chris   No. I mean on Sunday.

Frank   Well, I've got Sunday off.

Chris   I know. So have I.

Frank   Oh. Right.

Chris   You don't have to.

Frank   No. Yeah. Cool. OK.

Chris   Really?

Frank   Yeah.

Chris   Thank you.

Frank   Don't be silly.

Chris   OK.

Frank   You want my number then, or . . . ?

Chris   Got it off the rosters.

Frank   Right. Well. It's a date.

Chris *smiles.*

Frank   Well, not a . . . but. Yeah. I better be er . . . Yeah, see ya.

Frank *exits.*

Chris *takes in the view, smiles.*

Blackout.

Scene Four

The staffroom. The day after Scene Three. Wednesday evening. The TV is off.

Frank *is sitting reading a book.*

Enter **Mamta***, who goes to her coat to check her phone.*

Mamta   Hiya.

She smiles. **Frank** *continues reading.*

Mamta   You alright?

Frank *gives her a quick look.*

Mamta   Just seeing if I've got any messages.

Frank *goes back to reading.*

Mamta   Can't believe some of the customers today. First day here and I'm like: urgh. They make me wanna be sick. Though, I'm not anorexic or anything. Just allergic to the General Public, I think. I don't really put on weight. I'm an ectomorph apparently, just burn it off. (*Pause.*) I'm. Mamta. I just started. It's my first day. Today. Hello.

Frank   Right.

Mamta   And you're . . . Frank?

Frank   Apparently.

Mamta   Martin said, he was saying you went to uni, in Nottingham. I've got / family in . . .

Frank   I left. Dropped out.

Mamta   Well, I've got family. Own a restaurant in Nottingham, in the city centre. It's called the Palace. D'ya know it?

Frank   No.

Mamta   Oh, well, it's good. Really good. Won awards and stuff. If you ever go back, let us know and I'll put in a good word for you. Discount or whatever.

Frank, *still reading, shrugs vaguely.*

Mamta *receives a text.*

Mamta   Ooh, here we go. (*Reads the text.*) It's a joke. What drugs do ducks take?

Frank *looks at her briefly.*

Mamta   Quack.

She smiles at **Frank**, *pleadingly.*

Mamta   No takers? Yeah, that is a bit rubbish. It's not from my mates or anything. They're *slightly* funnier than that. I get sent these random texts. From this weird number. Like jokes and chart positions. D'you get them?

Frank No.

Mamta Well. Probably. Different network or like, something . . . tedious.

She smiles, flatly. Puts her phone back in her coat.

So, do you . . . do you know any, any good jokes?

Frank Yeah.

Mamta I'm all ears.

Frank You ever see a black kid on a bus?

Mamta What? Sorry, what d'ya say? Cos my hearing's a bit. I'm deaf in one ear. So I can't actually be all ears. Shouldn't really use that phrase, should I? Fell off a swing when I was three, landed really badly. So now I'm a bit . . .

She rolls up her tongue in her bottom lip, does a 'spastic' face and groan, as well as the requisite shaky, twisted-out hand movements. Then relaxes back to normal, smiling with a mixture of silly pride and embarrassment. A pause. She does the 'spastic' face/groan/hands again, just to fill the silence. Again, she finds herself quite funny/embarrassing.

(*Normal voice.*) Sorry. (*Reverting to the 'spastic' voice/posture.*) Sorry. Deaf in this ear. (*Another 'spastic' groan before going back to her normal voice.*) Sorry, I shouldn't really do that, should I? Bit wrong. Completely wrong, really. Something I do with my friends. The voice and the. But not usually with people I've just, I've just met. So, what was your joke? Something about a kid on a bus?

Frank *has found himself smirking at* **Mamta**'s *shtick.*

Frank Alright. Alright. Here's one for ya. How many feminists does it take to change a light bulb?

Mamta Erm. Dunno.

Frank Two. One to do it. One to suck my cock.

Mamta *smiles.*

Mamta   I like that. That's good. Erm. OK. Why do women wear make-up and perfume?

Frank   No idea.

Mamta   Cos they're ugly and they smell.

Frank *nods his approval.*

Frank   Not bad. Alright. Try this one. What's the difference between Patrick Kielty and a vagina that can't read?

Mamta *considers.*

Mamta   Oh shit. I know this, I've heard this. God, what was it? Oh, this is gonna kill me. Erm. Hang on. No, hang on. It's coming.

She twists her face up, trying to remember the punchline. **Frank** *smiles in anticipation.*

Mamta   Has it got anything to do with the fact that he's Irish?

Frank *shakes his head.*

Mamta   Oh. Shame.

Blackout.

Scene Five

A club: 'Lava & Ignite'. The day after Scene Four. Late Thursday evening.

Frank *and* **Emma** *at the bar, people-watching, looking over a dance floor.*

Emma   God. This place. Makes me feel like my hymen's grown back. Got your sights set?

Frank   What?

Emma   Got your eye on any ladies?

Frank   Not really.

Emma   You must of got loads at uni. All those hormones. Bet you couldn't move for . . . (*conjuring the imagery, failing*) . . . minge. Get much?

Frank   Can't say I did, to be honest.

Emma   How come?

Frank   Well, they were all a bit *young* and. Posh. Good-looking, yeah, but in that horrible plastic way, you know? All fucking bangles and stupid hair.

Emma   So you don't regret it then? Leaving?

Frank   No. I just, I just wanted so much for it to be. Better. You know? I mean, there were so many books there. Whole library. Whole world to learn about. But all these *kids* with their cliquey little gangs, they'd rather. They'd rather get pissed up on cheap vodka and dance like a twat to Abba in some overpriced warehouse.

Emma   What's wrong with Abba?

Frank   What?

Emma   Good band, Abba. Great tunes. Can't argue with great tunes.

Frank   Well, I'm not because, because that's not really my point, is it? My point is –

Emma   And I like cheap vodka. Gets you pissed dead quick.

Frank   *Emma*.

Emma   Yeah, calm down, alright? I'm just pulling your chain, Jesus. (*Pause.*) I was gonna go. Uni. Got the A levels for it. Did all the open days, interviews, got a place n' that

Frank   Oh, right. Doin' . . . ?

Emma   Law.

Frank   Shit.

Emma   Yeah, can you not sound quite so surprised?

Frank   Sorry, I just didn't know you . . .

Emma   Just cos I talk a bit rough don't mean I'm not an intellectual fucking powerhouse, alright? Anyway, I didn't go in the end, did I?

Frank   Why not?

Emma   Well. Mainly, primarily, it was because I couldn't really be arsed.

Frank *laughs.* **Emma** *joins in.*

Emma   Ooh. Hang on. You just got a look. Green strappy top. Eleven o'clock.

Frank *works out the clock and spots Green Top on the dance floor.*

Emma   She proper clocked you then.

Frank (*noticing her, but not interested*)   Did she?

Emma   You should get in there. Looks keen.

Frank (*dismissive*)   Got funny eyes.

Emma (*matter-of-fact*)   Good bum though.

They watch her dance.

Imagine hanging out the back of that. Be alright.

Frank   Well, you couldn't do it facing her.

Emma   Ooh, here we go. You see him? Black guy with the, with the silver earring. He's circling. Giving it the old. Tenner says he goes for her within two drinks. If you don't.

She gives him a knowing look, telling him off for not going and doing something about it.

Go on. Open goal there. Before he gets it.

Frank   Na, I'm alright, thanks. What about you? Spotted anyone?

Emma   Don't think any of these boys are ready to see me naked. Shock'd kill 'em.

Frank   Well, I didn't have no complaints.

Emma   Frank.

Frank   What? I didn't. All seemed very much in working order.

He smiles at **Emma***, who smiles back, a little embarrassed, before checking her phone for messages.*

Frank   Fancy some shots then or . . . ?

Emma   Nah. Gonna head off. Tell you what though, you should go over there and just straight out ask for her number. Mean it. Bet he won't. He'll just go for the grope. Being all . . . black.

Frank   Emma. Emma. If I said that, if I said that, you'd have a fucking *eppy*.

Emma   Shut up, I'm only mucking about. Don't mean it.

Frank   The shit I get . . .

Emma (*stern*)   Frank. Let's not, yeah?

Silence.

You seen that new girl? Just started? (*Pause.*) You gonna leave her be?

Frank   What?

Emma   I said, are you gonna leave her alone? Cos I swear if you say anything to her, I'll . . . Just don't, yeah?

Frank   OK. (*Pause.*) You want me . . . get us a, a taxi then? If you wanna go 'n that?

Emma   No need.

Frank   No?

Emma   I'm fine.

Frank   How come?

Emma   Make my own way. Got a lift.

Frank   Right.

Emma *smiles, not entirely convincingly, checks her messages again.*

Pause.

Frank   Got the anniversary coming up. Next month.

Emma   Of?

Frank   You know. Dad. Passing on.

Emma   God. Didn't realise. Sorry, mate.

Frank   Well, you know. Fuck it. It's alright. It's not like I knew him or anything, is it?

Emma   Still.

Frank   Yeah. Anniversary's always a bit. Weird more than anything. *(Pause.)* Sure you don't want just some shots or . . . ? Just like, one for the road?

Emma   Yeah. Best not.

Frank   Come on. Not drinking on my own.

Emma *starts to write a text message but is simultaneously looking over her phone at Green Top.*

Emma   Well, you don't have to. Look. She's talking about you with her mate. Sussing out if you're with me or not. Go on, go over now whilst she's still looking at ya. I can distract . . . him. I'm a great Wing Man.

She sends message, puts her phone away.

Frank   Fuck that.

Emma   Oh well, ta very much. Alright, fuck it, one more drink. What you having?

Frank   Guinness and black.

Emma   I told ya, I'm not ordering that. Two words: gay and, er . . . (*Pretending not to be able to find the word, then, as if suddenly enlightened.*) Oh yeah, gay.

Frank   Alright, I'll have a Carlsberg. Fascist.

Emma   Ooh, look. There we go. (*Facing Green Top's direction.*) *Told ya.* Our black friend wins. You lose. Look at his hands. Gone right up. And she's let him. (*Pause.*) Dirty cow.

They watch them kiss.

Blackout.

Scene Six

A week later. Thursday afternoon. A storeroom in the cinema. **Mamta** *is on the floor, rummaging through a cardboard box.*

Frank *is behind her with a pen and clipboard.*

Mamta   Fifteen. Seventeen. Eighteen. (*Pause.*) Eighteen Minstrels. Plus four, five. Five Fruit Pastilles.

Frank   Bang on. (*Notes it down.*) What about the Maltesers? Do them, we're pretty much done.

Mamta   Just a sec.

She pulls another box nearer. Starts going through it.

Fuck sake.

Frank   What?

Mamta   They've all. Split. But they don't look too bad. You hungry?

Frank (*after looking round to make sure no one is about*)   Yeah, fuck it, do the honours.

Mamta *reaches in. Pulls out a handful of loose Maltesers. Shares them with* **Frank**.

Frank   Cheers.

Mamta   'S alright. (*Back to the stocktake. With her mouth full.*)
Three, five. God. Are yours . . . ? A bit . . . stale?

Frank (*also with his mouth full*)   No, they're alright. How many
full packs are there?

Mamta   Erm. Nine.

Frank (*noting it down*)   Fucking hell. Actually . . . they're . . .
fucking . . .

Mamta *grabs a nearby small empty cardboard box and spits her
mouthful of Maltesers into it.*

Mamta   Ugh. Here you go.

She offers him the box. He takes it and spits out the Maltesers.

You alright?

Frank   Not sure I should say this out loud but. We have had
a bit of a rat problem.

Mamta   Really?

Frank *nods.*

Mamta   Is that what that tangy taste is?

Frank *nods.*

Frank   Why I tend to eat from sealed packs.

Mamta   God. I might, I might actually be sick.

Frank   No you won't.

Mamta *can't control herself and is sick into the box containing
Maltesers.*

Frank   Or. Maybe, you will.

Mamta   Ugh. / Ugh.

Frank   You alright? Want some water or summat?

Mamta *nods.*

Frank *goes.*

Mamta *gags and dry-vomits. Tries to force more sick out but can't. Tries to control her breathing, pulls her hair out of her face. Exhales deeply.*

Frank *returns with a glass of water for her. She takes it.*

Frank   It's cold.

Mamta *takes a sip.*

Mamta (*referring to the Maltesers*)   Think we might have to write those off.

Frank   I reckon.

Mamta   And you're also lucky cos I happen to look very sexy when I'm vomiting.

Frank   I can see that. Really brings out your eyes. Like. Literally. You want more water?

Mamta   No, I'm good. Thank you, though.

Frank   And you've got some, on you. On your . . .

He gestures to her top.

Mamta   Oh, that's, that's nasty. That's. That's never gonna come out.

She licks her thumb and starts to rub it off, which she continues to do through the next section of speech.

Oh God. You know. If we were in a fifties film and you were Jimmy Stewart and I was Katharine Hepburn, you'd have pointed it out, then wiped it clean with your hanky. Though cos it's the fifties it wouldn't be sick. It would be cake or. Something. And then our eyes'd meet after. And we'd. Kiss.

Pause.

Frank   How about I just get you another top?

Mamta   OK.

Frank *goes.*

Mamta *tries to seal down the lid of the box (the one she's been sick in), but the flaps keep coming back up.*

Mamta   Fucking. Stop it.

Pause. **Frank** *returns with a top.*

Frank   Here you go. Got a big one, just to be safe. I'm not saying you're fat or anything.

Throws the top to her. **Frank** *then turns round, with his back to her.*

Mamta   Thanks.

Frank   I'll make sure no one's coming.

Mamta   . . .

She changes her top as she talks to him.

Martin. Martin was, talking about me maybe taking a supervisor role on.

Frank   Already?

Mamta   What? Do you think it'd be too soon?

Frank   No, it's just. Watch him. Martin. He's a bit of a. Lech. Bit of a 'C' word.

Mamta   'C' word?

Frank   Cunt.

Mamta   Oh. He seemed alright. Quite. Sweet.

She puts her old top in the box she's been sick in.

Frank   Yeah, he does at first.

Mamta   So do ya think I should take it?

Frank   Do what you like.

Mamta   Be good for my CV. Before uni. So. And it's better pay. Makes sense. I think I fancy you.

Pause.

Frank   What?

Mamta   I know you're not meant to say that outright to someone. And Emma was saying she doesn't think that you like me or anything, and she's clearly right by the fact that you're not saying anything. So it doesn't matter that I said it, does it? We can just forget it and talk about something else.

Pause. **Frank** *turns to face her.*

Frank   To be honest. I'll be honest. You're not really. My type.

Mamta   Was it the being sick thing? Because I barely ever throw up. Unless I eat crab.

Frank (*smiling a little*)   No. We'll just. We'll just leave it at that. Alright? You're not. My type.

Mamta   I like that you don't say everything that you're thinking. It's nice, that. Some people just keep talking and talking about everything and anything, don't they? But you don't. I like that.

Frank   Yeah.

Mamta   Loads.

Mamta *takes one of* **Frank***'s hands.*

Pause.

Frank   What you doing?

Mamta   Holding your hand.

Frank   Why?

Mamta   Do you not like it? (*Pause.*) You don't like it?

Frank   What d'you reckon?

Mamta   I don't know.

Frank   Well, I do. I don't need you. (*Pulling his hand back.*) Touching me.

Mamta   What?

Frank   You heard. You ain't that deaf.

Mamta   What did I do . . . wrong? What?

Frank   And. And. You. You. Been here, been here five, five fucking minutes, think you can be my boss now?

Mamta   *No*. It got offered me. I was just asking your opinion. I mean. You turned it down. Martin said. So they need *someone* to −

Frank   Been here, what, two weeks?

Mamta   It's not exactly a difficult job, is it?

Frank *shakes his head.*

Frank   Almost had me for a bit.

Mamta   Had you?

Frank   Thinking you're. Alright. Different. But. Look at ya.

Mamta   You said it was OK.

Frank   Well, *it's not*.

Mamta   Why not?

Frank   God, you fucking reek of sick. You know that? Your mouth. Dirty. Look at it. Don't ya? *Reek*.

Mamta   Jesus. Why are you being such a . . . ? Knob now?

Frank   Sorry, boss, is that not allowed? Speak my fucking mind? Bother you that much, yeah? Hearing the fucking truth.

Mamta *shakes her head.*

Mamta   I don't. I don't understand what you're . . . doing. If you just, tell me. I'll listen. Promise. Whatever it is.

She looks at him, desperate to find an answer.

OK. Fine.

She exits.

Frank (*after her but under his breath*)   Yeah, go on. Piss off, you fucking . . .

He can't say the word.

Blackout.

Part Two

Scene One

April. A small room upstairs in the cinema. **Emma** *and* **Mamta** *are sitting at one side of the room. They are filling out forms.* **Frank** *is sitting at the other side of the room. He has a small bottle of water.*

Emma *and* **Frank** *both wear the normal cinema uniform.* **Mamta** *is wearing a shirt, as she is now kiosk supervisor.*

Mamta (*to* **Frank**) Would you like to talk through what happened?

No response.

Emma Just say what happened. Just get it over.

No response.

Frank.

No response.

Frank.

Mamta It might be better if you started this.

Frank *takes a sip of water.*

Emma Frank.

Mamta No, let him. This will get written down. He's shooting his own foot off.

Frank Nicely put.

Emma Frank.

Mamta Do you want to just talk through what happened? That might make it easier. And quicker.

Frank *scoffs instinctively and looks at* **Mamta**, *incredulous at her tone.*

Frank I find this pretty *extraordinary*, actually. When Pete was on bar, turned up *hammered* and set fire to the kitchen, he got a quiet word. How come I'm getting a *bollocking* / for – ?

Mamta   Frank. I didn't deal with that. Martin did. I wasn't here then.

Frank   What, did he tell you about it, over breakfast?

Emma   *Frank.*

Mamta (*abrupt*)   Why were you *smoking* in the *foyer*?

Frank *attempts to contain his rage, takes a big in-breath and takes another sip of water.*

Frank   Alright. OK. Alright. Had a big night. Alright? Feeling a bit like, nauseous. Like, I'm gonna be sick. So. I'm on my way to the toilet. I see Chris and he's having a cheeky cigarette in the foyer. While I'm there. Ask him for a drag. That's all. Which will settle me, my stomach. As I'm having it, you walk past. That simple.

Mamta   It's not quite that simple.

Frank   Well, it's not complicated. I smoke, or I puke in the popcorn. You want me to do a flow chart? I. Had a fag. With Chris.

Mamta   Yes. But. Chris had a coat on. Chris was on a break. Chris wasn't smoking in front of customers, wearing his uniform. About to go back and handle food, which he would then serve to those same customers. (*Pause.*) Have I got that wrong, at all?

Frank   You know that shirt quite suits ya. Brings out your eyes.

Mamta   Technically, this does deserve a written warning.

Frank   Is that. Are you serious?

Emma   Mamta, can we just . . . ?

Mamta   What?

Emma   I just don't think. This is a bit . . . you know?

Mamta   I am actually going to leave this as a verbal warning. It'll only stay on his record for six months. I'm doing him a favour.

Frank   If it's verbal, why are you writing things down?

Mamta   Well, there needs to be some record.

Frank   Of a verbal warning?

Mamta   Yeah. So we know that whatever you do next, you know, merits a written warning. Cos of the cumulative. Effect.

Frank   Can you not just, remember? Surely if it's written down and it's a warning . . . ? Then, technically – fucking *literally* – it's a written warning.

Mamta   If you've got nothing else to say . . .

Frank   I've got an absolute . . . *legion* of things to say.

Mamta   Well, that's partly why I haven't let this go.

Emma   Let's just. Chill out, yeah?

Pause.

Frank (*half sings, under his breath*)   Brown girl in the ring. Da, da da da da.

Mamta   What?

Emma   He doesn't mean . . .

Mamta   What are / you . . . ?

Frank   What? Boney M.

Emma *looks at* **Frank**, *pleading.*

Mamta   Have you got anything else – *relevant* – to add?

Frank   Do you not like disco?

Emma   Frank.

Frank   D'ya prefer bhangra?

Emma   Shut the fuck up.

Frank   Cos, I don't wanna stereotype or nothing. Lot o' your lot into hip hop, in't they? Like a solidarity, like *empathy* with black, oppressed culture thing. You gotta respect that, yeah?

No? Sorry, am I, am I out of turn? Am I not being, am I not being PC enough? Cos if I'm not just tell me and I'll. Keep it. Shtum. Promise. Cross my fucking. Just get confused about what I can and can't say these days, you know? Gets difficult to know where the line is. (*Pause.*) But then maybe, maybe you're right, maybe I should be a bit more careful with my phrasing on this kind of issue. Cos a better man than me, once said: 'Every idle word that men shall speak, they shall give account thereof in the day of judgement.' Every idle word. Imagine that. Everything that you've ever said and you'd have to stand there and defend it. Now. As an idea. That's. It's. Mental. But also. Brilliant. Do you not think?

No response.

Well, duty calls, I got nachos to prepare.

He stands and exits.

Mamta How can you stay friends with . . . ? (*She gestures after* **Frank**.)

Emma He's just. Ignore him, yeah? He's just a bit . . . upset. It was. You should know like . . . you know I said his dad died. Well, yesterday was the . . . the anniversary. And he was, he was drinking last night. A lot. On his own. To help him . . . get over it, you know? He was a marine, I think, and he, he drowned on some operation or summat before, before Frank was born. So, it's made things pretty hard for him, yeah? His mum's still a wreck about it and every year she goes a bit . . .

Mamta Right. OK.

Awkward pause.

Emma Do you want me to, to write that all up?

Mamta If you don't mind.

Emma What do you want me to put?

Mamta Just. Say that he was . . . *cooperative*. Whatever. Keep it vague. Put it in my pigeonhole. And I'll, I'll give it to Martin tomorrow.

Emma   Yeah.

Mamta   Thanks, Em.

Emma   Yeah.

She goes to leave, stops.

Just wanna say. Thanks. For not kicking off. I know he can be a shit. He's got no right. And. Just so you know. People call me Emma. Not Em.

She tries a smile and exits.

A pause before **Mamta** *notices some dirt on her sleeve, licks her thumb and tries to scratch it off.*

Blackout.

Scene Two

Later that day. **Frank** *and* **Chris**, *by the delivery doors. They are playing Dictators Top Trumps.*

Frank   Right. Height.

Chris   Musso . . . lini. Five foot eight.

Frank   Idi Amin. Six foot four. Give it.

Chris *passes card to* **Frank**.

Frank   OK. Erm. Countries invaded.

Chris   Vlad the . . . Im-parlour.

Frank   No, no, it's Vlad the Impaler.

Chris   Who was that?

Frank   Mad Russian bastard.

Chris (*nods*)   Countres invaded. One.

Frank   And here's another one. Stalin. Ten. Sorry, mate.

Chris *passes the card to* **Frank**.

Frank   Length of reign.

Chris   Fidel . . . Cas . . . tro. Forty-five years.

Frank *passes card to* **Chris**, *who reads it.*

Chris   Who is that?

Frank   Pinochet. Bloke from Chile. Army fella, bit of a shit. You want a cig?

He takes out packet of Marlboro Lights.

Chris   No.

Frank *offers cigarette.*

Frank   No?

Chris (*unsure*)   OK, yes.

He doesn't take one.

Frank   You don't have to.

Chris   OK.

Frank   It's your choice, mate.

Chris (*deciding*)   I won't.

Frank   OK. Good on ya.

Chris   I have been practising but they make my throat dry.

Frank *accepts the explanation and puts the cigarette in his mouth, while casually searching his pockets for a lighter.*

Chris   Facial hair.

Frank   George W. Bush. None.

Chris   Saddam Hussein. (*Smiles.*) Three.

Frank *passes card to* **Chris**. **Frank** *hasn't found a lighter.*

Chris   I've got some matches if you want.

Frank   You know what? Fuck 'em.

Puts the cigarette behind his ear.

Good little game, this. Where do you get 'em from?

Chris   Internet. Length of reign.

Frank   Ceauşescu. Twenty-four.

Chris *passes card to* **Frank**.

Chris   Here.

Frank (*looking at the card*)   Hello. Is that Pol Pot? Didn't know he looked like that. Nice little face.

He screws up his face and holds up the Pol Pot card next to his face, doing a little show for **Chris** *and putting on a 'Chinky' accent.*

Chinky-wink. Chinky chow-wow wing-wang wow-pow. Me love you long time, sucky-sucky? Five dollar. *Five dollar*. FIVE DOLLAR.

Chris *laughs.*

Frank   Sucky-sucky?

Emma *enters.*

Frank (*not having seen* **Emma**)   Sucky-sucky?

Emma   You alright, boys? Having a good time?

Chris   Yeah, we are.

Emma (*to* **Chris**, *referring to* **Frank**)   How's the big man?

Frank (*to* **Emma**, *referring to* **Mamta**)   She speaks to me again.

Emma   You said that without moving your lips. / Amazing.

Frank   Pete set fire to half of upstairs, always stealing. Fucking. Stinks.

Chris   I like Pete.

Emma   She's just trying to, to piss out her territory.

Chris   Pete's funny.

Frank   So why's she pissing on me?

Chris   But he does smell. Which category? / Frank?

Emma   Because you need to cut out all the . . . disco . . .
bollocks. That's not good, mate. At all.

Chris   What's disco bollocks?

Frank   Body count.

Chris   Is there a disco?

Frank   I said, body count.

Chris   Robert . . . Magoo . . . bee. A hundred thousand.

Frank *passes card to* **Chris**.

Emma   I just wanted to. You know. Make sure we're alright.

Frank   Yeah. Course we are. (*Pause.*) You. Um. Fancy getting
a drink in tonight?

Emma   Er. Yeah, OK.

Chris   Height.

Frank   We can. Just have a chat or . . .

Emma   Alright.

Chris   What height?

Frank   Be good, yeah.

Emma   And you know what, fuck her, you know? She's just.
She's a blatant, like, Little Hitler.

Chris   He was five foot eight. (*Gestures to the cards.*) Adolf
Hitler. Not that little.

Emma   Right. Thank you, Chris. Well. Fun as this is, I'll
be . . .

She motions that she is leaving.

Frank   Cool. Yeah.

Emma   See ya later.

Frank   We'll get a taxi. Yeah?

Emma   OK. I'll book it now. See you later, Chris.

No response from **Chris**, *who is looking at his cards.* **Emma** *exits.*

Chris   Height.

Frank   What?

Chris   What height?

Frank   Right. Kim Jong-Il. Approx. Five foot two.

Chris (*smiling*)   Have you made that up? Stupid, name.

Frank (*distracted, throwaway*)   Don't be a twat, course not.

The insult hangs in the air and **Chris** *buries himself in the cards.*
Silence.

Frank   Well? What you got?

Chris   She's just being nice.

Frank   What?

Chris   She doesn't fancy you.

Frank   Are you drunk?

Chris   I heard her.

Frank   Do wanna play this or what?

Chris   What.

Pause.

Frank   Wha' she say?

Chris   She's got a man. And she really likes him. He's in the army, like your dad was. She told Mamta. I heard them. He's called Paul. But she calls him Big Paul.

Frank   She chats all kindsa shit, yeah? You've got it wrong, yeah?

Chris   I'm not a liar.

Pause.

Frank   What else she say?

Chris   She told Mamta that you had a thing. I heard them. A little one-off fling, Emma said. But it was only cos she was so drunk.

Frank   You've completely. You're a little fucking . . . *and* it was more than once, so that's just . . . you're just wrong.

Chris   She said . . . that.

Frank *gestures for him to say more.*

Chris   She said that . . . she just felt sorry for you, just cos of what happened to your dad. She said it was a. (*Pause.*) Sympathy. Fuck.

Silence.

Frank   Chris.

Chris *offers his card to* **Frank**, *who doesn't take it.*

Silence.

Frank *places his cards neatly on the ground. Takes the cigarette from behind his ear. Presents it.*

Frank   Eat it.

Chris   What?

Frank   You heard.

Chris   Don't. That's horrible. No.

Frank   All of it. Right down. Now.

A moment. **Frank** *pounces violently on* **Chris**. *Pins him, struggling, to the floor. Forces open his mouth. Rams the cigarette in, despite* **Chris**'s *spluttering and struggling. Forces* **Chris**'s *mouth shut.*

Frank   Swallow. Is that a problem? Is that a fucking problem? Your throat too dry?

Chris *nods frantically.*

Frank   Well, that is a shame. WHAT. A. FUCKING. PITY.

Blackout.

Scene Three

The next morning. **Emma**'s *room.* **Frank** *and* **Emma** *are sitting on her bed.* **Emma** *is in a dressing gown.* **Frank** *is just in his boxers.*

Frank   Don't think I'm gonna go in today. My head's.

Emma   Yeah?

Frank   We can go into town. If you want. Get some lunch or . . .

Emma   I'm not. Not all that hungry.

Frank   Right. (*Pause.*) I like your room. Nice . . . layout. (*Pause.*) Was it OK, that we didn't use a . . . ? Like, is that gonna be OK?

Emma   Doesn't . . . matter.

Frank   Are you on the . . . ?

Emma   Yeah.

Pause.

Frank   Are you, erm . . . are you alright?

Emma   Yeah. fine.

Frank   You just seem a bit . . . (*Pause.*) I heard that you're . . . is it right that you're . . . seeing someone?

Pause. **Emma** *nods.*

Frank   How long? How long for?

Emma   'Bout, two months.

Frank   Is it . . . serious then or . . . ?

Emma (*shrugs*)   I like him, yeah. And he's not . . . better than you or anything. If you're thinking that. He's just. Decent, you know? I know it sounds shitty but . . .

Frank   Will I get to meet him?

Emma   Frank.

Frank   I know, I'm just . . .

Emma *digs out a packet of cigarettes.*

Frank   Thought you give up.

Emma *offers* **Frank** *one, he declines.* **Emma** *has a cigarette.*
Frank *watches her.*

Emma   You know, I think, I think Chris might just have a bit
of a crush on you.

No response.

Bet you twenty quid I'm right.

No response.

We can't do this again, yeah?

Frank   I know.

Emma   This is, like. I don't want this to happen every time
we . . .

Frank   Yeah.

Emma   You know? Because it could really mess things up for
me if Paul finds out and . . .

Frank   Yeah, I know how it goes. It's fine.

Emma   So we should probably stop going. For drinks and
stuff.

Frank *nods.*

Pause.

Emma   Thanks. For . . .

Frank   What?

Emma   Being cool with that.

Pause.

Frank   You're right by the way. About Chris. He does have a, a crush on me. Well. Did have.

Emma   Did have? What happened?

Pause.

Frank   Nothing. I just. Set him straight.

Emma   Bless him.

Frank   Yeah.

Silence.

Emma   Think I might have a shower. Go to work.

Frank   . . .

Emma   So . . . could you go? So I can have one?

Pause. **Frank** *nods.*

Emma   Thank you.

Neither of them moves.

Blackout.

Scene Four

Later, the same day. Early evening. **Frank** *is sitting on the steps of a large church in the centre of town. Wearing the same clothes. Deep in thought.*

Enter **Mamta**. *She is wearing a long red coat, which has a floral design, and is holding various shopping bags. She puts these down as she approaches* **Frank**.

Mamta   Thought it was you. Saw you from the high street. (*Pause.*) Look. I know you're probably just wanting me to go away already but I thought I should just come over and say hi. (*Pause.*) Hi. (*Pause.*) Is this your church? It's. Huge. Isn't it? Pillars and. Must be dead old. Never been inside. Always see it walking past. Sometimes have my lunch here on the steps but. Never gone in. What's it like? Inside? (*Pause.*) Are you not meant to be at work today?

Frank *looks up at her.*

Mamta   Have you called in sick or . . . ? What ya doing?

Frank   Thinking. What you doing?

Mamta   Shopping. Then I'm meeting my brother for dinner. We're going for Thai. Are you gonna make a joke about that? Something about Thai brides or ladyboys or . . . ?

Frank   Are you gonna tell anyone? Like Martin? That you saw me?

Mamta   You look awful.

Frank (*sarcastic*)   Thanks. Are you?

Mamta   I'm sure they'll cope.

Frank (*surprised*)   Right. (*Genuine.*) Thank you.

Mamta   Look tired. Should try and get a bit more. Sleep. When you're. Upset. Look like you might need it. (*Pause.*) Alright. OK, I'll leave you to it.

She goes to go.

Frank   Why am I . . . why am I upset?

Mamta   Because. You look it.

Frank   I look *shit*, I don't look *upset*.

Mamta   Sorry, I was. Just trying to help.

Frank   Help?

Mamta   Yeah.

Frank   Help what?

Mamta   Your. Situation.

Frank *stares at her, searchingly.*

Mamta   Cos of. Your dad. I don't know how I'd cope with that, I really don't. I mean the whole anniversary thing every year must be . . . awful.

Frank   Shame about your coat. Nice design but. Red and brown. Clashes.

Mamta   *Frank.* Who are you saying that for?

Frank   What?

Mamta   Yeah, well, I'm sorry, you can't play me like I'm fresh off the boat. I'm from St Albans.

Frank   That doesn't change a thing.

Mamta   What do you mean?

Frank   Just that. Right. Your lot, back home, got the caste thing, yeah? Which is like. Light at the top. Then darker as you get further down. Well, that ain't too far, give or take, from my way of thinking. Just give it a bit of a Doppler shift and you're there. But . . .

Mamta   But what?

Frank   But it's bigger than that, yeah? Where I'm coming from.

Mamta   Well, OK. I'm all ears.

Frank   You sure? Yeah? *Yeah?* Alright. Alright. Moses right? Moses, yeah? Moses saved the Hebrews, yeah? Jews. Led 'em out. But. This is the trick. Hebrew was a misprint. The original – listen, *listen*, yeah? – the original, the original translation, was, was 'hapiru'. H-A-P-I-R-U. Meaning. Light-skinned. Literally, that's all it means. 'Hapiru'. And they were the ones pulled out of Egypt. So the light, you see, the light were saved. And the dark, they drowned. Yeah? So, wind it back, wind it back, it's not a tribe, not Jews, it's people. White people. We were. We are. *Chosen.* So that's why the world is what it is.

Mamta   And what is it?

Frank   Right. You see a black kid on a bus, yeah? If he's on his own. Do an experiment for me. I mean it. Try this. Watch him, yeah? Young black kid, yeah? Watch him come up the stairs. First. First thing. Wass he do? He looks round. Quick. Straight away. Choosing where he's gonna sit. Yeah? Now, what's he looking for? I'll tell ya. Other black kids. *The threat.* He can't see me. I'm nothing. Like air, yeah? Like fucking. Tippex. Cos he's looking for them. He's looking for trouble.

Mamta   Have you rehearsed that?

Frank   No, but the little black kid has. Save him getting stabbed. Save him getting Damilola Taylor'd. Save him from. Trying to be safe in this country. That's what it takes.

Mamta   Two words. Jamie. Bulger.

Frank   Alright. Fuck that. Brixton. Riots.

Mamta   OK. Er. Police. Brutality.

Frank   Fuck off. History. Africa.

Mamta   You fuck off. Slave. Trade.

Frank   Feisty, in't ya? But I think you'll find there was a fairly prosperous, *historic* – fuck it, *prehistoric* – trade in that before we got there. We just redirected it. Made a bit o' dollar. And don't tell me, you see 'em in the paper, on telly, down in London, their self-created little ghettos, stabbing and shooting each other up, you *care. Fuck that.* You. Just glad it ain't you. Glad they keep it themselves. What's the phrase? Black on black.

Mamta   I do care. Don't –

Frank (*genuine*)   Darling, I don't believe you. As long as they keep it to themselves, you really don't give a fuck. Honestly, you don't –

Mamta   Frank, I'm not –

Frank   Now, I mean, you might wank on about it for appearance sake like all the other cunts. Like, blame it on the government. Or, or the media. Police. Or . . . legacy of

Empire. But let's fucking face it, where's the poor white kids
shooting each other up over the next shipment of crack
coming in? Where the fuck are they, yeah? Where's the white
kids setting up a whole genre of music so they can rap on about
what hateful fucking animals they are?

Mamta   Frank, that's mental, you're . . .

Frank   OK. OK. Alright. OK. History lesson, yeah? Back in
the day, India, motherland, whenever they had a revolt. British
Army, British Army would sew up any rioter inside a pig-skin
and fire 'em out of a cannon. Over the crowd. To get the
message across. To the locals. Teach 'em right from wrong.
Now, now it weren't right, was it? Was it? It was wrong.
Completely. And we've apologised for it, ain't we? But. Right.
Think about it, it's no different that, no different, to what your
lot are doing *now*. To their own. No different. We've civilised.
Got law. Respect it. Obey it. But your lot. All over. India.
Pakistan. Kashmir. Like the tenth fucking circle. Or, or, if
I wanna pull out the heavyweights. Sudan. Congo. You go
deepest, darkest. Fuck it, you look at any non-white country.
It's immense. Makes us, our fuck-ups, look like a cherry picnic.
Makes me look like a fucking saint. So, who had to pitch in
Kosovo? Sierra Leone? Who pitched in? Was it Nigeria? Was
it Egypt? India? Bangladesh? Was it fuck. It was us. My lot.
Me. Cos really, you don't give a fuck about a million dark faces
over there, do ya? You're the fucking racist. Suffering. Death.
Screams of a continent. Cos I'm white, you care more about
what I *say* than what all those billions of black and brown
fuckers actually *do*. To each other. To themselves. Now. Why is
that? Do you wanna know why?

Mamta *shakes her head in disbelief.*

Frank   Two reasons. First off, you know deep down that I'm
better than you. So you expect more. Demand more. Second
off, you're past caring. Cos it's just black on black. Whole
countries, but still, it's the same principle. Let's just leave 'em
to it, let 'em wipe each other out. Like. You've got to this
country, yeah? Posh area. White area. Nice school.

Mamta   Frank . . .

Frank   *White school.* So you've left it all behind, ain't ya?
And that's why we got on first off. Because you've embraced
me and what I think. (*Pause.*) Now I mean, I know you've got
all these liberal good intentions and off-the-shelf morals and
you're there, you're there looking down at me now, like I'm,
some kind of . . . monster, but actually, honestly. Be honest
with yourself. Just for one second. Because, let's face it, just like
everybody else you don't care about anyone or anything that
doesn't directly benefit you or people like you. Cos if you did,
you wouldn't be here now. You'd be out there doing something
to make things better for these people. So. When it comes
down to it. Now we've talked it all through. It turns out, you
think and feel exactly like I do. Exactly. It's just that I've got
the heart and the balls to say it out loud.

Silence.

Mamta   Are you done?

Frank *nods.*

Mamta   You know. I hope. (*Referring to the the church.*) If your
God is in there, I really hope He can hear you. All this.

Frank   Me too.

Mamta   I mean. Does talking like that, all that, speaking like
this to me, does that give you a boner / or – ?

Frank   No. Why, does it get you wet?

Mamta   Charming. Really. I can see why Emma went for
you. Or was it cos she was too drunk to stand up?

Frank   You're not funny, yeah?

Mamta   I fucking am. What's black and eats bananas? Half
of London. What do you call a dead Paki? A good start. Don't
be thinking you can shock me, alright? Or push me around.
Fucking . . . lecture me. You know the funny thing is, you
actually sound a bit like my dad. He was always saying stuff
like that. Like, doesn't matter who I marry as long as they're

not either black or Muslim and he'll rant on about everything
that happened back in Uganda. So actually as well as being
wrong, you're also being. Very. Deeply. Unoriginal. (*Pause.*) But
I think, I think some people need to keep talking like you do.
Cos if they stopped they'd realise that, God, I've got. Nothing.
The only way I can function is by directing all this shit out at
other people. Because if I stopped. If I stopped doing it for
one second and looked at my life. And was truly honest with
myself, I'd have to take the nearest knife and stab myself in the
heart. (*Pause.*) And. And d'ya know what's really funny?

Frank   What?

Mamta   Having listened to you now, I do think Emma was
genuinely mad for letting you and your tiny white cock
anywhere near her.

Pausing briefly for effect, **Mamta** *picks up her shopping and exits.*
Frank *watches her go.*

Blackout.

Scene Five

*We hear rainfall. Gradually at first but it soon becomes torrential. As the
sound eventually fades, lights come up on –*

Later that night. The garden of **Chris***'s family home.* **Frank** *is
standing out on the patio in the dark.* **Frank***'s face is bloodied and
bruised, particularly around his nose. There is also blood on his hands
and his top. He is breathing heavily, noisily, and has clearly been crying.
He is a mess, soaked through with rain.* **Chris** *is inside, wearing
pyjamas, a dressing gown and slippers, having just turned the living-room
light on. Both* **Frank** *and* **Chris** *are holding mobile phones to their ears.*

Having only just turned the light on, **Chris** *sees* **Frank** *for the first
time, through the glass of the locked patio door.*

They look at each other.

Chris (*talking to the mobile rather than* **Frank**)   What are you
doing in my garden?

No response.

It's late.

No response.

(*Looking directly at* **Frank**.) I was in bed.

Chris *lowers the mobile phone and places it in his dressing-gown pocket.* **Frank** *lowers his too, pockets it, as* **Chris** *unlocks the door with a key and comes out onto the patio, making sure he locks the door behind him.*

Chris   What do you want?

Frank   Can I . . . could I just . . . can I come in, yeah?

Chris (*shaking his head*)   Not allowed visitors.

Frank   Just . . . just for a bit, yeah?

Chris   Mum and Dad are very strict.

Frank   Just . . .

Chris   And you're not even very nice, so . . .

Frank   Chris.

Chris   So just . . .

Silence.

What happened to your face?

Frank   So you won't . . . ?

Chris   Looks sore.

Frank   Can we not . . . can we not just . . . talk? For a bit. Inside, yeah? It'll be fine, it will. I promise. I won't hurt you or . . . I mean, I mean we could just go up to your room and . . . and just . . . talk. Play cards or . . .

Chris *shakes his head.*

Frank   I just wanna. I just wanna clean up. Get warm. Dry. *Chris.*

Chris   Then go to your own house. Your own room.

Frank   Chris. I'm so cold, yeah? I'm . . . I'm . . . Fuck sake,
I'll be ten minutes, five minutes. Tops. I just need to clean up.
Look at me, for fuck sake. Look at me.

Chris   I am. But you can't. That's not . . . It's not fair.

Frank   Chris.

Chris   And what even happened to your face?

Frank   . . .

Chris   Why is there blood?

Frank   It's . . . it's nothing, yeah? I'm just . . . I fell over and,
and . . .

Chris   If it was nothing then you wouldn't be on my patio
late at night crying.

Frank   I'm . . . Look, look, alright, it was Mamta, yeah? It
was. Mamta. Mamta. She . . . I . . . I was . . . I followed her,
yeah?

Chris   I don't believe anything you say anyway, so . . .

Frank   Look, I told you I . . . I followed her and . . .

Chris (*hushed, so as not to wake anyone*)   Frank, I don't care what
you say, *you're not coming in my house so you can just . . . go.*

Frank *looks at* **Chris** *and takes a second to slow down/control his
breathing.*

Frank   Right. (*Pause.*) She was with her, her brother. In town.
They had dinner together, but . . . then, then he left. So, she
was, she was on her own. And I . . . I follow her. (*Pause.*) I watch
her go down off the high street and she . . . gets her bus. Then.
Quickly like, I sneak on after. (*Pause.*) So, so she's upstairs and
I'm down, downstairs, at the back. Tucked away, and I'm
watching. Waiting. For like ten, twenty minutes. Eventually,
we stop and she comes down. I watch her, watch her slow, like
slow motion, coming down, wearing this coat, this red coat,
down the stairs, through the doors, off. And she still ain't seen
me. Fucking. Oblivious. So I go. Follow. Just slip through the

doors. Driver says summat behind me but I don't hear him. Can't. Just. Focus. And I go. (*Pause.*) Then, suddenly I'm. Was very. Very. Quiet. Dark. I'm on the street and it's. Quiet. Empty. And I thought. And I thought. I watched her walking ahead of me, away from me, and I thought. Yeah. Yeah. (*Pause.*) So I got her. I just ran quick and I got her. Easy. Lift her up. Catch her. Lift her up off the street. And I, I put her down hard in this, this alley. And she's struggling and screaming but I, I shut her up, yeah? Quick. I hit her, yeah? Like reaction, like. Her face. Hit her. And she screams, like. So, so I hit her 'gain. But she jumps up. Jumps for me. Goes for me. And this punch, like she gets this one, like, this one lucky punch at me, yeah? Lunge, gets me here and I'm straight off, bleeding. So I'm shocked, yeah? Hurt. But the punch. Just made it worse, yeah? Made me worse, yeah? Then I. When she did that I just. Then I just. Lost it. Got her down with this kick in her stomach, then these punches coming over and over, quick, then this last one, like this kick when she's down. In her. Into her. I kick her and. I mean, her neck, it. It just. It just. Broke. Snap. And her eyes . . . her eyes were . . . gone.

Chris   Gone?

Frank *nods.*

Frank   Heard it. Her neck. And her eyes were . . .

Chris   So you . . . ? You're saying that you . . . ?

Frank *nods.*

Frank   And I hold her. Her body. I pick her up and I rest her on me. She ain't breathing and I can feel the weight of her on me, her body. And I take one of her arms and I hold it in my hand. Feel the weight of it. Look at it. Then I take it and I push it, I push it down on this railing behind her. And the spike, the railing, it comes up, through, like through the wrist. And she don't scream or . . . so she must be . . . and it's actually . . . easy. To do that. You wouldn't think. To push it down, through it. But it is. Easy. (*Pause.*) So I take her other arm. Do the same. Push it down on this railing. It comes up through it. See her blood. Bone. Metal. And I've done it now

so she's, she's hanging there. Like. Cross. Like a. A cross. She's
there. And then I . . . She's there, so I . . . I touch her. My
hand in her jeans, feel her. She's still warm. Soft. Wet. (*Pause.*)
And then I . . .

Silence.

Chris   You're so . . . horrible.

Frank *nods.*

Chris   Why do you . . . ? (*Pause.*) I don't understand why . . .

Pause. **Frank** *starts to back away.*

Chris   Where are you going?

Frank *edges further away.*

Chris   Where are you going, Frank?

Pause.

Frank   Away.

Frank *exits.*

Chris (*after him*)   Frank? (*Pause.*) Frank.

A moment.

Blackout.

Scene Six

*Early evening, the next day. The lights fade up on the staffroom at the
cinema.* **Emma** *is eating and watching a* Sopranos *video.*

Enter **Mamta***, coming in to get her coat and purse.*

Mamta   You alright?

Emma   Yeah, cool. Just. You know.

Mamta   I'm off to McDonald's, want anything?

Emma (*gestures to her salad, which is in a Tupperware container on
her lap*)   Nah, I'm alright, thanks.

Mamta   You had a good day?

Emma   Magic.

Mamta   I've been completely 'argh'. Feet are killing me. This gyppo guy, this idiot. Tells me women shouldn't get to be managers. Cos I won't let his nine-year-old into an eighteen. They've always got a chip on their shoulder, apparently. Women.

Emma   Yeah. My uncle says that.

Mamta   Right. God. Is he a wanker?

Emma   No, he's my uncle. (*Pause.*) Have you seen Frank about?

Mamta   Yeah. I meant to tell you, actually.

Emma   What?

As **Mamta** *pauses,* **Emma** *mutes the TV. A brief silence.*

Mamta   Met him in town. This is. Yesterday. I tried to be nice. Make things alright. Went over to him. Really made the effort. But. He started being all. All in my face. And. We had a few . . . words. He was being an absolute *arse*. All this racist shit.

Emma   I'm sorry. He's such a. We had a . . . *relapse* after we went for a drink the other night, and I, I shouldn't have. I know that. So. Then I told him. That we couldn't like. See each other. Or . . . So he was probably still. Upset.

Mamta   Why are you making . . . excuses for him?

Emma   I'm not. I'm just saying. He just takes stuff out on people. And this time it was . . . it was you, you know?

Mamta   It's not just been this one time.

Emma   I know. Fair point. But this whole thing with his dad's really fucked him up, you know? It makes him say stuff. Snap at people. He doesn't mean it. I can't believe that he can actually mean it. Saying all that. To you.

Mamta   Well, it sounded pretty convincing. And. What I don't get. At all. Is how can you sleep with someone who

comes out with stuff like that. The way he looks at me. Like
I'm . . .

Emma   It just. He's . . . / *nice.*

Mamta   Like I'm to blame for . . .

Emma   I know it's hard to . . . to justify. But. He can be so
lovely. So . . . soft. (*Pause.*) What did he say?

Mamta   He was giving it the full white-power shit. So. I
walked away. I wasn't gonna put up with that. Lower myself
to listen to that. Then, bit later, he came over, out of nowhere,
told me and my brother that I was up my own arse and that
I need a good lay to sort me out.

Emma   Right.

Mamta   And he said he'd heard that Gandhi was good in
bed and . . .

Emma   He's such a mong. I'm sorry.

Mamta   So my brother. Wasn't gonna take that. Knocked
him out. We were by the car park. Near the. Fire station. He'd
followed me. From the high street. Weirdo.

Emma   Did 'e hurt him?

Mamta   Busted his face up a bit. Kicked him. It was funny,
really, more than anything. Bit cartoony. All this blood. Didn't
look real. I think he was actually crying. But. We left him to it.
Went for dinner.

Emma   That's a bit . . . fucking . . .

Mamta   What?

Emma   *Harsh.* For saying Gandhi was . . . randy.

Mamta   That's not what he meant.

Emma   Yeah, but that's what he said. No wonder he hasn't
come back in.

Mamta   Well, he won't be. I've talked to Martin.

Emma (*shocked*)   *Have you?*

Mamta   Yeah.

Emma   You *punched* him, so you *sacked* him?

Mamta   That's not someone I want to work with.

Emma   Oh, and we couldn't have you being upset, could we?

Mamta   Are you still . . . are you still siding with him?

Emma   No, but *for fuck sake*. I know you're a good girl. But. I'm struggling to . . . (*Pause.*) Right. Frank talks a lot of *shit* but I never seen him *hit* anyone. Never seem him beat someone up in the street, leave 'em there to rot. Then laugh about it. Eating a fucking curry.

Mamta   It was Thai.

Emma   Whatever. You get Thai curry, don't ya?

Mamta   He'll be *fine*. It was just a few cuts, bit o' blood.

Emma   Mamta. Much as I feel for ya. For what he said. Which I'm sure was awful and spiteful and stupid. And it must be terrible to hear that. And I know I could never know what that's like. Hearing that. But. (*Pause.*) I'm not sure I can jump up and down with joy knowing my mate's had his face kicked in by your idiot brother. I don't think that's *fine*.

Mamta   Mate?

Emma   Yeah, mate.

Mamta   Even now?

Emma   Yeah.

Mamta   That's pretty . . . shit.

Emma   Maybe it is. So what?

Mamta   So what?

Emma   Yeah. I mean, what gives you the right to be so fucking . . . high and mighty? Have you looked in the mirror lately?

Mamta   I haven't done anything.

Emma   Oh, fuck that. Fuck. That. You watch and laugh as Frank gets beat up. You manage everyone here like they're fucking retards or summat.

Mamta   Well, look. Everyone here acts like. Trash. So that's how I'm gonna treat 'em. Simple as that. That's how it works. People fuck around, I'm not gonna put up with it, some fake smile. I mean, how do you want me to treat everyone? Like they're all my best mate?

Emma   *No*. Just. With a bit of *respect*, yeah? (*Pause*.) I'll tell you what, though. I'll tell ya summat for nothing. The more I listen to you, the more it all makes sense. Cos, you know, all my worst experiences in clubs, bars, have been. Asian guys. Yeah? Calling me a white . . . whatever. Threatening ya. Grabbing up ya skirt. Pushing ya round. Treating ya like cheap meat.

Mamta   OK. But I've seen the way you dress, Emma, when you're going out, and maybe there's a reason for that.

Emma   Yeah, well, I think it's a different kinda reason, but I won't say it out loud, case ya get your brother in here, beat fuck out me.

Mamta   Could be a good idea.

Emma   Oh yeah?

Mamta   Yeah. (*Pause*.) But for now. I'll tell you what. I'll tell *you* something. I'm going out to get some food. Then I'm gonna go for a bit of a walk. Bit of fresh air. So I'll be off for about half an hour. When I get back. I want you gone. Or if not, I'll get security to do it.

Emma   You what?

Mamta   You heard.

They look at each other.

Emma   Well, I may as well save you the walk.

She stands, calmly collects her coat and bag. As she gets to the door, she turns and looks one last time at **Mamta**.

Emma   And you know what else? I don't believe in God, yeah? Heaven. Hell. Or any of that stuff that Frank does. (*Pause.*) But I do hope, sincerely, that you *fucking burn.*

Silence.

She exits.

A pause before **Mamta** *takes a seat.*

Blackout.

Scene Seven

By the delivery doors, which are closed. A few hours after Scene Five. **Frank** *is sitting on the ground in a heap.*

Silence.

Enter **Chris**.

Chris   Thought you'd be here.

Frank   I'm not. I'm really not. I'm not anywhere, mate.

Chris   I got this at the garage.

Chris *takes a can of Diet Coke from his coat pocket and offers it to* **Frank**. **Frank** *looks at* **Chris** *for a second before taking the can gratefully. As they talk,* **Frank** *opens the can and drinks from it.*

Frank   I just didn't know where to go.

Chris   Alright.

Frank   I'm an adult.

Chris   I called Mamta.

Frank   And the place I run to is . . .

Chris   To make sure that she was OK.

Frank   I couldn't think of anywhere else.

Chris   And she was. Apart from being annoyed I woke her up.

Frank   Coming from town, first thing I saw. Light from the gyppos' campfire.

Chris   But it's OK, I didn't tell her what you said about her. Just said I got the wrong number. (*Pause.*) You are a rubbish liar.

Frank *takes out a crumpled pack of cigarettes. Takes out a bent cigarette, which is snapped in the middle.* **Frank** *has to push it together with his fingers to be able to smoke it successfully. He does so, lights it, takes a drag.*

Frank   Share it. Please.

He passes it.

Have to keep your fingers on it.

Chris *does so, smokes.* **Frank** *waits for a cough. It doesn't come.* **Frank** *smiles.*

Frank   I'm sorry, mate. I am.

Chris *offers back the cigarette.*

Chris   What for?

Frank *takes the cigarette.*

Frank   Why did you . . . why did you come here?

Chris   Don't know. Just did.

Pause.

Frank   What's the, what's the worst thing you've ever done?

Chris   We went camping in Scotland with my family once and I hid my sister's medicine and she went into a coma.

Frank   Fuck. How long for?

Chris   Eight weeks.

Frank   Shit.

Chris   What about you?

Frank   Don't even know.

Pause.

Chris   I bought you some face-wipes.

Frank (*confused*)   OK.

Chris *takes out the wipes.*

Chris   For your face.

Frank   What?

Chris   So you don't get infected.

A pause. **Chris** *takes out a wipe. He moves towards* **Frank***, who initially flinches as the wipe touches his face.* **Chris** *gently starts to clean* **Frank***'s face, which he tilts back, and continues to do so as they speak.*

Frank   Thank you.

Chris *nods.*

Pause.

Frank   You should probably ask me where I'm going on me holidays.

Pause.

Chris   Where are you going on your holidays?

Frank   Suppose it'll have to be here. (*Pause.*) What about you?

Chris   Alaska.

Frank   What?

Chris   Alaska. Like cold places. Snow. Mountains. And I like grizzly bears. Would like to see them. Catching salmon.

Frank   Reckon I'd look good with one of them hats. With the. Flaps.

Chris   Maybe.

Frank   Hunt for bears.

Chris   Yeah.

Silence apart from **Chris** *cleaning* **Frank**.

Chris   Kill them.

Frank *nods gently*.

Chris *stops cleaning, looks at* **Frank**, *before awkwardly leaning in and kissing him. Taken by the moment,* **Frank** *kisses him back.* **Chris** *puts his hand on* **Frank**'s *shoulders and pulls himself away from him, looking tenderly at* **Frank**'s *face.* **Frank** *looks down, evading eye contact.*

Frank   What do you even . . . like about me?

Chris   Your stretch marks.

Frank   What?

Chris   You were changing once and I saw them while you were pulling your top down. Like little lightning flashes. My sister hates hers, but I like yours.

A smile edges onto **Frank**'s *face before he successfully swallows it with a frown.*

Frank   I'm sorry, mate. But you shouldn't, look at me like that. That's not what I'm about.

Silence.

Chris   I saw your house today. (*Pause.*) After my shift, cos you was on the rota and I was a bit worried cos you never have days off. Thought you might be in trouble or . . . so I got your address off the taxi list. (*Pause.*) Took me ages to get there. I was on my bike and there was loads of country lanes to get over. And when I got there. (*Pause.*) Never seen a house that big. Least not on my estate. Had stables. And a gazebo. Thought I must have got the wrong house by being thick as usual or something. But a man answered your door and I asked him who he was and where you were and he said that he was your dad and that you were at the cinema. I told him I thought he was dead, though, and he asked me if I was on drugs or something and said he would call the police if I didn't get the fuck away from his house. So I left. Went home and just had a pizza.

Frank Chris.

Chris And then you turn up and claim all that rubbish about Mamta. Why are you such a *liar*? About everything? I mean, why do you pretend like you're poor and you did that thing to Mamta when . . . ?

Frank That's such a stupid question. You don't know anything. About me or *anything*. Little story, yeah?

Chris What story? / I asked a question.

Frank Shut up. Shut up, *listen*. *Listen*. Gehenna, right, Gehenna was the original word for Hell. You understand? *Hell*. And Gehenna was an actual place, like a valley where they sacrificed children. So, at the time scripture was like, be good or you'll be damned to go to what now would be, er, Dunblane or . . . Lockerbie. Somewhere shit, somewhere associated with death and fucking . . . evil. Yeah?

Chris What . . . like Corby?

Frank But they were wrong. It isn't even that far away. It never is. It isn't a valley somewhere. It isn't just fucking Corby, twat. It isn't removed from us in like a distant plain or place. Wherever you live, wherever you are, they're stood around us, like fucking demons. They live with us. Eat with us. Shit with us. Fucking. Everywhere. See 'em. You see 'em? And it's fucked to ignore that. Or think that I'm *lucky*. My house and my fucking . . . furnishings has got nothing to do with *me* or *what I am* or *what the world is*, you fucking *girl*.

Chris Do you wanna swap houses then? Cos I'd love to live in your house.

Frank Yeah, well then, you're completely fucked and missing the point.

Chris Prob'ly. But I don't think I'm the only one. Who is fucked.

Silence.

Can I have the can back, please? To recycle.

Frank *looks at him. Picks up the can, throws it at the feet of* **Chris**.

Chris   Thank you.

Frank   You're welcome.

Chris   I won't tell anyone you kissed me. They might think less of you. (*Pause.*) And I do think it's sad that you lie so much. I think it's prob'ly the saddest things in the whole world. (*Pause.*) Because I wanted so much to stay here. With you. On your lips. (*Pause.*) Like. For about a whole month I thought I was in love with you. (*Pause.*) I must be very, very stupid. More stupid than I even thought. (*Pause.*) But then at least I'm not as stupid as you.

He picks up the can of Diet Coke and puts it into his coat pocket.

Goodnight.

He exits.

Frank *watches him go.*

Silence.

Frank *takes out his lighter. Flicks it on and watches the flame. Does this a few times before putting his hand above the flame, feeling the heat until it becomes too much. He does this a few times, gradually breaking into a broad grin as he starts to savour the pain/sensation of it.*

Blackout.